I'M PREGNANT.

NOW WHAT?

CLEO STANLEY
AND
CAROLYN SIMPSON

ROSEN
PUBLISHING®

New York

Published in 2012 by The Rosen Publishing Group, Inc.
29 East 21st Street, New York, NY 10010

First Edition

Library of Congress Cataloging-in-Publication Data

Stanley, Cleo.
I'm pregnant, now what? / Cleo Stanley, Carolyn Simpson.—1st ed.
     p. cm.—(Teen life 411)
Includes bibliographical references and index.
ISBN 978-1-4488-4651-1 (library binding)
1. Teenage pregnancy—United States. 2. Teenage mothers—United States. I. Simpson, Carolyn. II. Title.
HQ759.4.S716 2012
618.200835—dc22

                                                              2010042038

Manufactured in the United States of America

CPSIA Compliance Information: Batch #S11YA: For further information, contact Rosen Publishing, New York, New York, at 1-800-237-9932.

Contents

According to statistics reported in January 2010 by the Guttmacher Institute (a nonprofit organization that works to educate the public about reproductive health research), teenage pregnancy rates are on the rise, after more than ten years of declining numbers. About 712,620 American teenagers between the ages of fifteen and nineteen became pregnant in 2005. That number increased by 3 percent in 2006 and 5 percent in 2007. Eighty-two percent of teen pregnancies are unplanned. Nearly two-thirds of all teen pregnancies occur among eighteen- to nineteen-year-olds, according to the Guttmacher Institute's report.

If a young woman has ever engaged in sex, she probably knows how accidents can happen. Perhaps the

According to data released in January 2010 by the Guttmacher Institute, a private nonprofit reproductive health research organization, 10 percent of all births in the United States are to teens.

young woman didn't mean to "go all the way." Perhaps she thought she would not become pregnant the first time. Maybe she just didn't want to think about it. Whatever the case, the first thing to do when a woman suspects she may be pregnant is to find out for sure.

Before you assume that you are pregnant, you need to confirm the pregnancy. The quickest way to do so is to use a home pregnancy test. These tests can be purchased at a drugstore or grocery store, and they are usually located in the personal hygiene section of the store. They can also be bought online. Test kits vary in price but usually cost less than $20.

Most home pregnancy tests are fairly easy to use. Typically, you merely urinate in a container, dip the test stick into the urine, and then watch for the color to change. You will know the results immediately. Depending on the test, one color means that you're pregnant; another means you're not. These tests are generally accurate even when the woman is only a few days late with her period. Many women like using the home tests because they can learn the results in private.

Some people prefer to visit a local family planning clinic to find out whether they are pregnant. Although these clinics use pregnancy tests similar to the home test kits, they can also test a person's blood for a hormone called human chorionic gonadotropin, or HCG. HCG shows up earlier in the bloodstream of pregnant women than it does in their urine.

Going to a family planning clinic has other advantages. Should a pregnancy be confirmed, the woman can talk with nurses and counselors about available options. Moreover, family planning clinics will treat teens without involving the teens' parents. Most will encourage young people to tell their parents that they are pregnant and will even help them break the news to them. Finally, family planning clinics will provide the person with information about financial resources if she decides to keep the baby.

It is important to confirm your pregnancy early because 1) you have more options available in the beginning of a pregnancy, and 2) you need to start prenatal care as soon as possible to ensure a healthy baby. Teenagers are especially at risk for low birth weight babies (infants who weigh less than 5.5 pounds [2.5 kilograms] at birth) and premature births.

The first part of this book can help you check out your options if you are (or someone you know is) pregnant. All the choices presented are legal, but moral considerations may make one alternative more acceptable to an individual than another. Readers can find information about helpful organizations and Web sites listed at the back of this book.

The rest of the book deals with the physical and emotional aspects of pregnancy, the birth experience, and the consequences. Should you decide to raise the child yourself or with the father, you can read about the resources available to you. Another chapter will present information to help you understand a baby's needs.

Two chapters on losses are included in the final section of the book because nearly 626,000 pregnancies are lost every year through miscarriage and stillbirth, according to the American Pregnancy Association. The stages of grief are described in the chapter about losing your baby, enabling you to recognize that you can survive this kind of heart-wrenching loss. Fortunately, most of you will not experience this kind of loss. The second chapter on loss provides information about a type of loss that you will share with others, and that is the loss of your own childhood. This is a loss that needs to be grieved, too.

The book's concluding chapter is on contraception, or birth control, so that people can plan for their next pregnancy. A woman's life is not over because she is pregnant. Teens who are pregnant need to know their options and where they can find encouragement and assistance. This book will help them in these quests.

CHAPTER 1

ADOPTION: AN OPTION FOR NOT KEEPING THE BABY

There are different types of adoption agencies where you can explore the option of giving up your baby to a family. At some private religious organizations, you can live without cost in a home for unwed mothers-to-be for the duration of your pregnancy. In some private adoption agencies, the adoptive couple covers the expenses of the pregnancy and delivery. In most cases, you will have nothing to do with your child once he or she has been handed over to the adoptive couple. For some, that may be just what you want: no further contact. For others, the very fact that you will never see your child grow up may keep you from the whole idea of adoption.

If you are considering adoption, explore your options (either privately or through the Department of Health and Human Services) at a family planning clinic. The professionals at these family planning clinics will explain the choices to you and refer you to the appropriate agencies. Most teens do not consider this alternative, although there are hundreds of suitable families that exist who would love to adopt a child.

Adoption was a far more acceptable alternative to motherhood decades ago. Perhaps because single parenthood has lost much of its stigma, adoption has lost favor in the eye of the general public. Some clinicians today believe that there is a greater stigma attached to giving up your baby than to raising the baby as a single parent. Of the women that coauthor Carolyn Simpson—a teacher, clinical social worker, therapist, and author in Oklahoma—has spoken with about this issue and many of the issues related in this book, most were adamant that they could not have given up their child.

Sharon is a young woman who chose to give up her baby for adoption. She stayed at a home that was run by the Catholic Church. She attended the mandatory groups and activities but mostly tried to stay by herself. Sharon's boyfriend wouldn't marry her, and Sharon knew she would not be able to provide for this baby without having family support.

Because her older sister had a baby out of wedlock, Sharon was fairly sure of her family's reaction to her being pregnant. Her mother would cry and carry on and inform everyone that she was not going to raise another baby herself. Maybe Sharon's mother would tell her to have an abortion. Sharon would refuse to do that; she considered it murder after having seen a television documentary on the subject. Her only alternative, as she saw it, was adoption. Maybe someone else would raise her baby the way she wished she could.

Sharon agonized over her choice. Unlike abortion, where the decision is made and irrevocable once

A counselor advises a teen who is pregnant about the options she has for giving up her baby for adoption. In forty U.S. states and the District of Columbia, a mother who is younger than eighteen can legally place her baby up for adoption without her parent's involvement.

the procedure has taken place, adoption is something you can reconsider all the way up to and past delivery. Sharon tried not to think about the baby growing inside her because it only made her decision to give him up more difficult. She pretended she was at the Catholic-run home because she was ill, an illness that would go away in a few more months.

After the birth, when she had signed away her rights as a parent (as her boyfriend, Jim, also had to do, as the baby's father), all she felt was an ugly rage at this guy who did not have to go through her ordeal.

Sharon said, "Jim never felt the baby move. He never stayed awake all night because the baby kept kicking his rib cage. He didn't have to go through anything physical, like I did. It just makes me so mad; it's so unfair. Maybe I'm really mad that I got trapped in this situation, but all I can feel right now is furious that I had to be the only one to suffer. Labor and delivery hurt more than I expected. Maybe if I had a husband and had known I was going to keep the baby, I wouldn't have minded so much. But I kept telling myself that the baby wasn't mine and the sooner the ordeal was over, the better."

Many of the women said they tried to feel as little as possible about the pregnancy. They refused to connect to the wonder of pregnancy the fact that they were carrying a life inside them because that would have made the impending loss so much greater.

"I didn't want to hear anyone talking about bonding or anything," one said. "I didn't want to feel life because ultimately I knew I'd be giving up this child, and if I didn't notice it in the first place, I wouldn't mind giving it up so much."

In these unfortunate circumstances, the woman usually feels cheated by participating in the miraculous process of birth but having nothing in the end.

It takes a truly high-minded person to give up her child because she is concerned for its happiness and health. When the woman knows she cannot provide for the child and wants her baby to have a good chance in life that adoptive parents could provide, she deserves at least to have peace of mind. Often, although she may be relieved, there is the ever-present sense of loss.

That sense of loss can be so overwhelming to both the mother and father that some have tried to regain custody of their child. A well-known case of this involved Baby Jessica. Jan and Robby DeBoer had to return custody of their adopted daughter, Jessica, to her biological parents. The biological mother had identified the wrong man as the father, so the real father—who had not known of the existence of his child—had not surrendered his parental rights. After years of court battles, the adoption was eventually reversed.

Another famous case is that of Baby Richard, who was almost four when his adoptive parents, the Warburtons, were forced to return him to his biological parents. In this case, the birth parents were not married and were having problems in their relationship. The biological mother, Daniela Janikova, not only refused to disclose Richard's father's identity to the adoptive parents, but she told the biological father that Richard had died. The biological father learned the truth a few months later. He and the mother eventually married, and they got their child back.

Another case involved twin sisters. When Cindy Ruiz found out she was pregnant with twins, she and

Colette and Jim Rost hug their adoptive twins after a court hearing. The courts approved a settlement giving the adoptive parents permanent custody of the twins after a lengthy custody battle that wrestled with Native American legal authority and the rights of adoptive and biological parents.

the father, Rick Adams, were not married. They knew they would not be able to take care of the babies and their two sons as well. When the twins were born, they gave custody to Colette and Jim Rost of Ohio. The twins were later discovered to be part Native American, an inheritance through the birth father's grandparents who are Pomo Indians. Those grandparents wanted custody of the baby girls to raise them in the Native American culture. Because the twins are part Native American, the adoption was subject to the federal Indian Child Welfare Act (established in 1978 to protect native culture) and not to state adoption laws. According to a 1997 report in the *Los Angeles Times*, the case went all the way to the U.S. Supreme Court before it was sent back to a lower court. Then the Adamses (Cindy and Rick got married) decided not to go through with the case. In the end, all parties reached a settlement, deciding in the best interest of the girls, who remained with the Rosts, the adoptive parents. The Adamses were given one-week visitation rights annually and received regular reports and phone calls about the twins' progress and well-being. The girls also learned about the Pomo Indians and Native American culture as part of the agreement.

The majority of the fifty-two thousand adoptions that occur yearly in the United States are without mishap, but a number of cases have involved legal problems or the biological parents changing their minds. The most unfortunate aspect of these cases is that, ultimately, the children are the victims. The custody battles often take so long that the babies are toddlers before a case is settled. If the courts decide to reverse the adoption, these children are taken from the only family they have ever known.

Adoption also means grieving "the child that might have been." As in any loss, there is denial of pain, anger, a sense of injustice, numbness, and grieving. Eventually come feelings of acceptance and resignation to the loss.

1. Have you looked into the various types of adoption agencies, and are you satisfied that what you're doing is best for you and the baby?
2. Can you live with the possibility of never seeing your child again?
3. Can you live with the reality that another woman will be "Mommy" to your child?
4. Are you willing to face the possibility that the child may look you up one day and not understand why you gave him or her away?
5. If you aren't ready for permanent adoption, have you considered temporary foster care?
6. Do you care that your boyfriend or his family might choose to adopt the baby themselves?

CONSIDERING ADOPTION

One girl told Simpson that she had never considered adoption because it would have been a "living death." She said, "I couldn't have stood the thought that someone else was raising my kid. What if they weren't nice to her? What if I changed my mind and wanted her back after all this time? What if my own kid hated me for giving her up?"

Melanie chose adoption because, as an abused child herself, she didn't think her family offered a decent environment for her baby. She stands by her decision to give up the baby, but from time to time she worries and wonders. "Sometimes I wonder," she said, "if his new parents are treating him OK. Sometimes I think if only I could be with him, I could keep him safe. But that's kind of stupid, isn't it? I couldn't even keep myself safe!"

Lorna is a woman in her thirties. When she was a freshman in college, she became pregnant by a guy she had known less than a month, so she chose to drop out of school for a while, have the baby, and give it up for adoption. No one at school knew except her roommates. Lorna returned the next semester and went on to finish her education, later becoming a successful lawyer. She said she has no regrets about the adoption, that she no longer wonders if her baby grew up well. Nonetheless, every October 25—the date of his birth—she falls into a mild but inconsolable depression.

If you think adoption might be the best choice for you and you've looked into the various resources to help you in that decision, be prepared to still feel some sadness.

It may be helpful, once you decide on this course of action, to write out a list of reasons why you cannot care for the baby yourself. List the reasons why giving up your baby to another couple would be in the baby's best interest. Keep the list with you, especially at delivery. Then if you choose to hold the baby and get caught up in the emotion of the moment, you can grab your list and remind yourself why keeping the baby just won't work.

Sometimes a woman changes her mind at delivery and keeps the baby, only to discover weeks later that she just cannot care for him. At that point, it is much more painful to give up the child.

Another option is temporary foster care, whereby you briefly give up your baby to another person's care. When you are in a better position to care for the child yourself, you can regain custody. You have not lost total parental rights, as you would if you chose adoption.

Foster care is disruptive to both you and the baby. It has its downside and upside, the downside being that you miss out on those early opportunities to bond with your child, and the upside being that you gain time to mature.

Believe it or not, the baby's father must sign the adoption papers, too, waiving his parental rights. Simpson knew of one woman who decided to give up her baby, only to learn in court that her former boyfriend's parents had asked to raise it. The court awarded the baby to them.

Few guys are willing to take the baby from the mother. Usually, the guy will let his girlfriend make that decision for both of them.

THE GUY'S VIEWPOINT

You, the guy, the father, will probably feel either relieved or upset, depending on how much you wanted the child. Although you may not want to pursue a relationship with the mother, you may still want to have contact with your baby. Perhaps your family may want to have contact with the child, and family members will pressure you not to relinquish your parental rights.

ADOPTION: HELPFUL TIPS FOR MAKING A DECISION

1. Consider your age and ability to care for a baby.
2. If you are uncertain about adoption, first look into foster care, which is temporary.
3. Discuss adoption with your family planning clinic, your doctor, or a social worker.
4. Talk to others who have given up children for adoption.
5. If you or the birth father are of Native American descent, remember that your child will be subject to the Child Welfare Act of 1978. Efforts will be made to place the child with other Native Americans of the same tribe, not necessarily a couple you have chosen.
6. Consider how much involvement you want in your child's life.
7. Sign up with an adoption group so that your child can eventually locate you if he or she wants (and if that is what you want).
8. List the reasons that you think adoption is best. Write them down and take them to the hospital with you. If you have second thoughts, pull out your list and read what you have written.
9. Realize that you will have second thoughts and grief.
10. Above all, consider the needs of the child. Write a letter to that child (to be opened when he or she is an adult) that explains your feelings.

If you do not consent to adoption, you need to have a frank discussion about your responsibilities to your child. It is not fair to anyone (especially the child) to reject adoption plans and then be unable to handle your financial and emotional responsibilities.

If you do agree with your girlfriend that adoption is the best path to choose, help her plan for it. If possible, agree to meet the prospective parents with her.

Keep them informed of your address so that the child can eventually find you if he or she desires. Remember, it is not only the birth mother the child wants to find later in life; it is the birth parents.

Most important, support your girlfriend through the birth process and afterward. You will both have second thoughts about what you're doing, but it's easier to do if you see it through together and encourage each other.

CHAPTER 2

MARRIAGE

In past generations, when a teenager found herself pregnant, she rushed to do the right thing, which was to marry the baby's father. These days, that pregnant teenager may be thirteen years old. Getting married at thirteen is rather unrealistic.

But let's say you are the pregnant teenager, and you have a good relationship with your boyfriend. How should you decide whether you should get married?

First, don't get married just because your parents will "kill you" if you don't. And don't get married just to give your baby a legitimate last name; you can give your baby your or your boyfriend's last name without even marrying him. You get married for several reasons, and although loving each other is a pretty good reason, it isn't enough.

GROUNDS FOR GETTING MARRIED

For most couples, there are many reasons for getting married. Usually, couples have more than one reason for entering into a lifetime commitment of marriage. The reasons may include the following:

1. Being the right age. Believe it or not, the most likely indicator of divorce is the age

of the marrying couple. The older the people are when they get married, the better the odds that the marriage will survive. People do so much growing and changing when they're in their teens and early twenties. Someone you love at thirteen may be entirely wrong for you at eighteen. Moreover, the person you were at thirteen is probably a lot different from the adult you become at eighteen. So, the first factor should be how old (and mature) you are. Older teens (who have more schooling) are in better positions to marry.

2. Having related interests and comparable backgrounds. Opposites may attract, but if you do not have similar values, interests, and experiences, you will not have much to sustain your marriage. That is not to say that teenagers with different ethnic backgrounds should not marry, but that diverse backgrounds (including different classes as well as races or religions) make for different expectations.

3. Being committed to the relationship. Having a stable relationship does not necessarily mean how many years you've been dating each other. It's not so much the years of togetherness that count—it's the level of commitment you have to that relationship. If you stay married, you will be looking at each other over the breakfast table for many years. Is this the person you want to see every day for the rest of your life?

If your relationship isn't solid, rethink marrying. You must be committed to the relationship, especially when the baby arrives, since you'll need to care for each other and the baby.

4. Consider, too, whether at least one of you has an income to provide for a family. If neither of you has a job, who is going to pay for a home and food? If you both think you could move in with one set of parents, is the parents' relationship unwavering, or are they having problems? Are there resources available to handle both an extra person and a baby?

5. Being reliable and having an eagerness to carry out responsibilities. You both must be responsible or the marriage won't work. Both partners need to handle a great deal of responsibility if they are going to provide financial and emotional support to each other and to the baby. Good partners make good parents; they are conscientious, trustworthy, dependable, and mature, and they can put others' needs ahead of their own at times instead of acting impulsively.

6. Having help whether or not you reside with your parents. Sometimes parents do not or cannot provide financial support to teens. Make sure you have other means of support. Perhaps you and your boyfriend have jobs or have relatives who are willing to help you. You need to find out about agencies or programs that can provide aid to teen parents. Family planning clinics and houses of worship are good choices for support.

Think about all these variables before considering marriage. It is a big commitment. If you're looking at divorce as being a safety net, you're not ready for marriage.

Divorce, even when the marriage is not worth saving, feels terrible. It hurts. It hurts to give up on something or someone you loved or still love. Divorce also brings many problems. You need to determine who gets custody of the child, figure out visiting time for the noncustodial parent, and determine financial support.

Jerome, Bonnie's boyfriend, was having trouble with his own family, so he moved in with Bonnie's family. He had his own room downstairs, but gradually Bonnie's parents stopped noticing how much time the two were spending together. Bonnie liked being with Jerome. Soon they became sexually active without considering the consequences. Bonnie later admitted that because they had always planned to marry, a pregnancy just didn't seem to be a significant issue. Bonnie did become pregnant.

CONSIDERING MARRIAGE

1. Is the father of your unborn child someone with whom you want to spend the next fifty years of your life?
2. How do you both feel about disciplining a child? Do you believe in spanking? In verbally threatening the child? Can you think of any circumstances in which you would strike your child?
3. What do you both think about earning, spending, and saving money?
4. Are you planning to stay at home with your child only temporarily? Do you both agree on when you should begin work? Will you need more education, and how will you get it?
5. How many children do you both want?
6. What type of family life have you both experienced?
7. How much family support do you have now?
8. How are you going to spend family holidays?
9. How flexible is your spouse-to-be?
10. How does he relate to children? How do you?

She was stunned, not believing that it would actually happen. Sometimes she tried to "wish it away," but when she finally accepted the pregnancy, she and her boyfriend chose to get married. Bonnie was certain marriage would make everything all right in the end.

SOME REMARKS ABOUT MARRIAGE CEREMONIES

Most young women are excited about the upcoming marriage and the wedding. Weddings are supposed to be the bride's special day; she gets presents, money, and lots of attention. But don't be surprised if you are worried ("What have I gotten myself into?"), angry ("Will I be missing out on something by getting married now— or to this guy?"), and even a little depressed ("Is my life over now? What if I've made a mistake?"). These feelings do not necessarily mean that you don't want to be married. Sometimes an event as significant as your wedding sobers you to the point of thinking about what you are doing. Although you may be perfectly thrilled to be marrying the guy you love, you may also realize that you're giving up some things. You will be a married woman and about to become a mother, with many responsibilities. The focus will soon shift from you to the baby you're carrying. In addition, when the newness wears off, you will still be living with this man, and you'll be a wife and a mother and will handle all the responsibilities that come with marriage and a family.

Second thoughts are not necessarily bad to have at this time. Listen to them because they are telling you that the changes in your life will take some adjustment and that what you are undertaking is important. However, do not base a change of heart on feeling "blue" for a while. It's a normal feeling.

HANDLING YOUR FEELINGS

Do not bottle up your feelings; it only makes the problem worse. It's OK to talk about having second thoughts, but be selective in sharing those thoughts. You don't

A pregnant bride and her groom pose for wedding photos. Even if you marry and go on a honeymoon, you still will have your pregnancy and baby to deal with afterward.

need some blabbermouth running around telling everyone that you're depressed about getting married. Choose a concerned adult who can help you put those feelings in perspective. Talk to a religious adviser at your house of worship or a trusted teacher.

Carolyn Simpson's former client had an unhappy experience with her own wedding. Rene had never aspired to a career. All she ever wanted out of life was the love of a good husband and several babies to raise. When she became pregnant at seventeen, it wasn't the end of the world. She had completed high school months before and knew she was involved with the man she wanted to marry. Unfortunately, as supportive as her parents were, they were ashamed of her pregnancy and wanted the wedding to take place with as little fanfare as possible.

Fearing that others were probably shaking their heads in disapproval, they sacrificed Rene's early excitement for a rushed ceremony. Rene, whose dream had always included a big church wedding, the white dress, and a pile of presents, had to be content with a ceremony conducted in her home. Her father walked her across the living room instead of down the aisle at church. Only her siblings and aunts and uncles witnessed the event. More distant family members were notified afterward. Rene, who is an unusually perceptive teenager, said to Simpson later, "By treating the whole ceremony so casually, they gave me the impression that I was being punished. That if I'd done things right, they would have gone out of their way to give me a big wedding. As it turned out, I felt like a criminal, doing something really dirty—so dirty that we couldn't invite the other relatives to watch it. Most of my family gave us wedding presents, but it wasn't the same as having a surprise shower. I felt the disapproval that came with every gift.

"For a long time afterward, I was really mad at my parents. I mean, you'd have thought they'd be understanding. After all, they had to get married themselves. I guess they just expected better of me. There, see? I'm starting to believe it myself: that I did something wrong or could have done better. I love my husband, and I already love this baby. What's so awful about that?"

Then again, sometimes the fancy wedding does take place. You get many presents, you're the focus of activity for days leading up to the big event and then the center of attention on the day itself. It's enough to make you lose sight of the fact that you're still pregnant and have to deal with that. The honeymoon is a weekend in another town in the ritziest hotel your dad can afford, and then on Monday reality hits when everyone starts planning for the baby. There's hardly any period of adjustment to married life. First there are the Lamaze classes so that you both know what will happen during childbirth. Then there's your mother telling you all the little things you need for a baby, including why drawstring-tied nightgowns are better than sleepers. Suddenly, there you are: barely a couple and with plans for a baby. It's hard not to feel cheated or jealous. You feel cheated for missing out on other "couple" activities, and jealous of this new life growing inside you. Try to keep the following points in mind:

1. Talk to your future spouse. Chances are he's feeling funny, too. Even if you both are nervous and worried, by sharing these feelings you may find yourselves drawn closer together.

2. If your decision to get married is a good one (and you have good criteria to help you decide), acknowledge your feelings and trust your instincts. No one is ever 100 percent sure of every major decision.

3. If your parents are contributing to your misery (perhaps treating you as if you are making the biggest mistake of your life), either tell them how you feel, or, better yet, enlist the support of another adult to tell them. Marriages can certainly survive the difficult circumstances in which they may start.

Remember, as long as you are honest with yourself and how you are feeling, your decision about whether or not to get married will be the right one for you.

THE GUY'S VIEWPOINT

Not all guys faint or wither away when the topic of marriage comes up. Although Simpson certainly has seen many more guys who felt they were too young to get married, some have gone to extraordinary measures to fulfill their responsibilities. Wayne was a young guy who worked with Simpson at a hospital some years ago. He had what Simpson called the "rescuer mentality."

Wayne had not dated much in high school. The ward clerk at the hospital—a girl of eighteen—became pregnant, and her boyfriend evaporated into thin air. Wayne started dating Nancy, even when others warned him that she might accuse him of being the father. When Nancy was in the last stages of pregnancy, Wayne asked her to marry him. In his determination to take responsibility for all of them, he had almost forgotten that the baby wasn't his. They married, Nancy quit work to stay home with the baby, and after the delivery Wayne was so proud that people might have thought he had done all the work himself.

Ed was another young man Simpson knew. He was dating a girl a year older than himself. When she went off to college one fall, he said, "If anything happens and you get pregnant or anything, you don't have to worry. I'll marry you in a second."

These were very supportive words coming from a young guy who was still in high school and had his college years ahead of him. The ironic thing was that he wasn't necessarily referring to her getting pregnant by him. No matter how she wound up in that condition, Ed was willing to assume all responsibility. Simpson's hunch is that Ed was caught up in the role of "knight in shining armor." He had no concept of how hard it is to finish high school, to work to pay bills, to love a woman (who might have become pregnant by somebody else), and then to support her child.

Some guys actually want to settle down, but it is a safe bet that most do not want a wife and child when they haven't even finished high school.

For you guys, perhaps it is not a matter of making your steady girlfriend pregnant. Perhaps it was a two-week affair with a girl you soon realized you did not care much about. Unfortunately, the relationship progressed so fast that intimacy developed before caring and love. In that case, the mere thought of marriage may turn your knees to jelly.

Some of you may be angry that your parents are making you do the "honorable" thing. Some may be resentful because you have to settle down and give up your partying days. Maybe you don't really care one way or the other because you think you can always get a divorce if things don't work out, or your wife will tolerate your fooling around anyway.

If you feel that way, you should not be getting married. Anyone who feels badgered into getting married makes a lousy spouse. And anyone who thinks divorce will save him two or three years down the line has no right to put his wife and child through that upheaval. If you don't want to get married, *don't*! No one can force you. Of course, you do have an obligation to support your child, but you do not have to marry the baby's mother to honor that obligation.

Nonetheless, you are as fully entitled to your second thoughts as your girlfriend. If you have both decided after careful consideration to get married, and you are basically happy but maybe a little worried and scared, share your thoughts and get on with things. It is only when you pretend your feelings don't count that they threaten to overwhelm you.

CHAPTER 3

BEING A SINGLE PARENT: AN OPTION TO GO IT ALONE

Bristol Palin, daughter of former Alaska governor Sarah Palin, made national news in 2008 when she announced her unplanned pregnancy at the age of seventeen during her mother's campaign for vice president of the United States. She and her boyfriend, Levi Johnston, originally planned to get married, but they later decided to go their separate ways. Bristol gave birth to a son, Tripp, and has been raising him as a single mother. Bristol now publicly advocates for abstinence-only sex education and speaks out about protecting unborn children and about the trials and tribulations of being a teen mother. Many people find her willingness to talk about preventing teen pregnancy and the difficulties of being a single parent encouraging.

What if you're pregnant, though? What if you are not in a position to marry your boyfriend or are no longer together, you refuse to have an abortion, and you cannot bear the thought of giving up your child for adoption, even temporarily to foster care? Your only remaining choice is to raise the baby yourself. That is a gloomy prospect for some teenagers, but certainly not for all.

The first reactions of some teenagers are shock and denial. "I can't be pregnant." "This isn't happening to me!" For whatever reason, the girl ignores the indisputable facts: the missed period, the swollen breasts, the morning nausea, the fatigue, and the mood swings. Either she avoids using a pregnancy test to confirm her suspicions, or she simply does not consider the possibility of pregnancy at all. It is hard to believe that anyone could be pregnant and not realize it, but it does happen. Sometimes it is a matter of ignorance: the girl does not realize that sex can lead to babies. Sometimes it is more a matter of not wanting to know.

Bristol Palin and her son, Tripp, are seen here between rehearsals for *Dancing with the Stars*. Palin, who was a celebrity contestant on the TV dance show, speaks about teen pregnancy and advocates sexual abstinence for unmarried teens.

DENYING THE PREGNANCY

No doubt you have heard the well-publicized stories of teenagers who hid their pregnancies and disposed of the baby after he or she was born. Amy Grossberg and Brian Peterson were two bright, young teenagers from wealthy families. When Amy became pregnant, they were afraid to tell their parents. However, they did nothing to end the pregnancy. Amy went into labor. Brian took her to a motel, where he helped her deliver their son. Police speculate that the baby was born alive. They suspect that the teenagers killed the infant, stuffed him in a trash bag, and left him in the dumpster outside the motel, where he was later found. Both teens returned to their colleges and pretended nothing had happened.

Another story involves Melissa Drexler, who delivered a baby in a bathroom stall at her high school prom. She, too, told no one about her pregnancy. After cleaning herself up and discarding the baby's body, she returned to the dance floor.

These teens denied their pregnancies not only to their families and friends but also to themselves. Fearing that their parents would be disappointed in them, they tried to keep the pregnancy a secret. In the end, they were frightened and desperate and did the unthinkable.

These stories underline the fact that denial is prevalent among teenagers and that it is very dangerous. The pregnancy does not go away by ignoring it; however, the opportunity to plan or prepare for the pregnancy does go away. Should you want to terminate the pregnancy, you lose valuable time by ignoring it. Even if you want to keep the baby, you can miss out on necessary prenatal care. Babies can die from lack of proper care and nutrition. During the forty weeks of pregnancy, it is important not only to avoid certain things (drugs, alcohol, and smoking), but also to give your body vitamins and nutritionally balanced meals.

PREGNANCY

Many women become pregnant because they don't know enough about how their bodies and reproductive systems work. A little more than a third of teenagers know when the fertile time of their cycle is each month. Simpson asked Jill, a sixteen-year-old mother, if she knew at what time of the month she was most likely to become pregnant. She replied, "Let's see, everyone has told me different things. I think fourteen days after your period, you can get pregnant. Or maybe it's fourteen days after your period you can't get pregnant. It's one of the two."

You can become pregnant only four to five days each month. However, it is imperative that you use birth control each and every time you engage in sex. How will you know when those four to five days occur? You can become pregnant only when you are ovulating. Ovulation is often hard to predict. The fourteen-day point is based on a twenty-eight-day cycle. Ovulation (barring unforeseen circumstances, such as stress or illness) occurs fourteen days before the start of your next period (ovulation often occurs around day fourteen of a woman's cycle, but this timing varies among women and can change from month to month), and you can become pregnant shortly before, during, and after ovulation. But how do you know ahead of time when your next period will start? A teenager is too new at the game of predicting menstrual cycles to take chances. Also, teenage girls often experience irregular menstrual cycles, which makes things even more confusing. Even for adults, it is often very difficult to predict ovulation. Be safe and use birth control. According to statistics reported by the Guttmacher Institute, a sexually active teenager who doesn't use birth control has a 90 percent chance of becoming pregnant within a year.

Sometimes birth control can surprise you, too. Karen was using the pill faithfully, though it didn't agree with her and she was constantly throwing up. Her doctor told her to stay with it a while longer to give her system a chance to get used to the extra hormones. What he neglected to tell her was to use some other form of birth control as well. Karen became pregnant, even when taking the pill every night.

Fanny never considered using birth control regularly, although she had taken a sex education course and knew that it was possible to become pregnant with just one unprotected act of sex. Unfortunately, she didn't think it would happen to her. She conceived at the age of sixteen.

In 2010, *U.S. News & World Report* announced that the American Academy of Pediatrics (AAP) had issued a policy statement endorsing a comprehensive sex education program in high schools. According to the AAP, children get more sex education from television, music videos, and the Internet than they do from their parents and teachers. The United States currently has the highest rate of teen pregnancies in the developed world. Pediatricians note that, clearly, an abstinence-only education has been ineffective. They recommend a comprehensive sex education program that is grounded in science, which they believe will better educate young people and prevent unwanted pregnancies.

The Guttmacher Institute reports that every year, nearly 750,000 young women between the ages of fifteen and nineteen become pregnant. Eighty-two percent of teen pregnancies are unplanned—these account for almost one-fifth of all unplanned pregnancies per year. However, the alarming news is an increase in the number of pregnant twelve- and thirteen-year-olds. These are the kids who believe an assortment of myths: "If I do it less than five times, I won't get pregnant." "If I stand up right after sex, I won't get pregnant." "If I do it during my period, I won't get pregnant." The truth is that you can get pregnant at age twelve for the same reason that you can get pregnant at age seventeen or thirty. Any act of unprotected sex can lead to pregnancy.

As with anything else, teenagers are often angry when they realize they are pregnant: angry to be in this predicament and have to make a decision, angry at the loss of control over their lives and the uncertain future.

Karen, the girl who had responsibly used the pill for birth control, found herself pregnant at the start of her senior year. A good athlete, she was looking forward to being captain of some of the teams. All that changed when she became pregnant; obviously she could not waddle down center court or run hurdles carrying an extra 30 pounds (13.6 kilograms).

SOME USEFUL ASSISTANCE

The back of this book lists some agencies that can help you prepare for and support your baby. They may be able to assist you with some of the following:

1. Filing for Medicaid and the Title V MCH Block Grant Program and Title XIX benefits to pay for your pre- and postnatal care.
2. Filing for Women, Infants, and Children (WIC) benefits and food stamps, which will entitle you and your baby to receive milk, milk products, peanut butter, whole grain bread, brown rice, juice, infant cereal, and many other food staples. Your baby is eligible for WIC up to the age of five.
3. Filing to get into low-cost government housing and to secure maternity clothes, baby clothes, furniture, and baby supplies. Often churches or religious organizations will help supply you with baby clothes, furniture, and diapers, too.

"I missed out on that year, and though I'm happy with my daughter now," she said, "I'll never get that year back." Other girls get bogged down worrying about how they will support a baby or survive labor and the physical uncertainties of pregnancy. For those of you who have neither a boyfriend nor family to rely on for support, nurses and social workers are available to work with you, as well as public assistance for prenatal care, housing, and counseling. Check with your community family planning clinic. People there should be able to provide you with contact information for a public health nurse and other agency resources. Don't waste time worrying. There is help out there, but you have to ask for it.

YOUR RESPONSE TO BEING PREGNANT

Along with anger and fear, some girls feel regret early in their pregnancy. Sometimes a girl really wants to become pregnant more or less to see if she has the ability to conceive. Then when she has conceived, she panics and thinks, "Oh no, what have I done?" She realizes at this point that she won't be buying that dress for the spring prom. She won't be playing Juliet in the senior play when she's two weeks short of delivery. It's rather like seeing your life pass before your eyes, only in this case it's all the missed opportunities that rush past, not the memories.

Not everyone is "struck down" by pregnancy, as unanticipated as the event may be. Some girls told Simpson that they were thrilled when they realized they were pregnant. It was an accomplishment; it marked their emergence into adulthood. These girls usually had easy, nausea-free pregnancies, and they felt their "glow" throughout the nine months. It was something they either wanted or welcomed.

Sometimes the good feelings are based on the assumption that the unborn baby will give you unconditional love. Actually, textbooks will tell you that only parents and dogs can give "unconditional" love—or love that is given no matter what comes back in return. (Note, however, that not all parents are capable themselves of giving unconditional love.) But a baby will not fulfill your wish to be loved. And the infant has the opposite idea, anyway: that you are there to fulfill his or her need to be loved and cared for. It is not until a child is much older that he or she may try to give you something back.

Randi was fifteen when she discovered she was pregnant. She was thrilled, even though she knew she would be raising the baby herself. Her boyfriend had joined the air force before the pregnancy test turned up positive. Randi's father had left the family when she was two. Her mother had died when Randi was ten, and now she lived alternately with an older brother and an older married sister. To Randi, it always seemed that everyone left her or pushed her away. Now that she was pregnant, she reasoned, she would have someone—the baby—who would always be there, always be hers.

Shawna was another girl who felt isolated from kids at school. She was scared of the popular girls because she didn't think she measured up to them. Shawna didn't have their money or nice clothes. But when she became pregnant, that no longer mattered. She felt special because she was doing something mature, something that meant someone had found her desirable. Shawna told Simpson about the time she was walking downtown and spotted a group of the popular girls hanging out in front of the drugstore.

Shawna said, "Before, I would have been too scared to walk past them. I would have figured they were all watching me, making fun of my clothes or the way I walked. This time I didn't care. I sailed right on by them. I even said hi. I just wanted to shout, 'Hey, look at me. I'm going to be a mother. So who cares what I'm wearing?' It was a great feeling. I felt powerful, having made a baby and all."

At the other end of the spectrum, you may be feeling embarrassed over your blossoming pregnancy. Though people of an earlier generation seemed to have more hang-ups—more things that caused them to squirm with embarrassment—teenagers today still may be uncomfortable with their condition, especially if they continue to go to school. There's nothing like asking permission to go to the bathroom three times in one class, sitting two feet away from the desk because you're too pregnant to get any closer. In those cases, you might be happy about the pregnancy, but your dignity got left behind along the way.

Not surprisingly, pregnant teenagers can become depressed when they contemplate the turn their life has taken. Depression (feeling down, blue, sad) is merely anger turned on yourself. It encompasses hopelessness, futility, and at the extreme end, thoughts of suicide. "What am I going to do? I can't have this baby. My Dad will kill me if he finds out."

Periods of depression are not uncommon for a girl suddenly facing an unplanned pregnancy. The pregnancy itself accounts for some of the "down" times because your hormones are all out of whack. It's OK to be discouraged, sad, or blue; it's even normal.

CONSIDERING SINGLE PARENTHOOD

1. How much do you know about infants?
2. Do you have any real-life experience with them?
3. Do you have any adult to turn to if you become overwhelmed when things don't go as planned?
4. How do you plan to calm a cranky baby?
5. How will you maintain a social life?
6. Where will you live, and how will you support yourself and your child? For how long?
7. What hobbies or interests do you have? How will you maintain them?
8. How will you see to it that your baby gets adequate medical care?
9. What will you do if you're not a good mother?
10. Do you know CPR and the Heimlich maneuver? Can you handle a medical emergency?

What is not OK is when your feelings don't lift or your thoughts turn to serious plans to hurt yourself. Suicidal thoughts, even if you have no concrete plan of action, need immediate attention by a trained professional. Call a suicide hotline, a counseling agency, your minister or rabbi, your doctor, the hospital, or the police. Don't think you have to go through this alone, and don't think it's a sign of character to endure every crisis on your own. It's a sign of strength to know when you need help. Your life is out of control right now, and it's hard to make any decision, let alone the right one. Never be afraid to seek out a concerned adult.

If you plan to face parenthood without a partner, you can lessen the shock by beefing up your support system. The most successful parents (whether they are married or not) are those who have their parents' support and encouragement. Being pregnant and then raising a child is demanding work, both in time and money. Your parents have already been through all this; let them help you now. If they can't, check out resources from your house of worship or local family planning clinic.

If your boyfriend failed to come through, don't think the situation is unmanageable. It will just be a bit more challenging.

THE GUY'S VIEWPOINT

Although your girlfriend may opt to have this baby herself, you certainly have feelings about the whole situation. Some guys are relieved that they are not going to be pushed into a marriage they don't want. They mistakenly believe that their responsibilities ended when their girlfriend got pregnant. If you're one of them—relieved not to concern yourself anymore with the pregnancy or child—you are in for a rude awakening. Your responsibility does not end. If fact, it won't end for at least another eighteen years.

You, as the father, are responsible for child support until the child is eighteen years old. Even if you are not married to the child's mother, even if it was only a one-night stand, you are still responsible. If the child's

These teen parents attend a high school class with their children. A father is legally responsible for his child's financial support until the child turns eighteen, even if he doesn't marry the child's mother.

mother applies for Temporary Assistance for Needy Families (TANF), which is administered by the Office of Family Assistance (part of the Department of Health and Human Services), she may not get it unless she names you as the father. Then the government is entitled to take part of your wages for child support. So, although you may be relieved that you will not be involved in the day-to-day care and raising of the baby, realize that you must still support him or her financially.

You may be confused when your girlfriend tells you she's pregnant: "What am I supposed to do now?" Rich is one who first felt that way. He had known Mia only a few months and had dated her for two weeks before discovering that they had little in common. In fact, he didn't even like her very much. Several weeks after they broke up, Mia caught up with him running to class.

"I'm pregnant," she told him. "What are you going to do about it?"

Rich was shocked. He knew there was good reason for her to be pregnant by him, but he could not believe it was happening because he didn't like her anymore.

Rich suggested an abortion. Mia wouldn't hear of it. He explained that he had no intention of marrying her, so she said, "I'll raise the baby myself then."

Mia was immediately kicked out of her home. Rich, feeling responsible (especially when he discovered she was only fifteen, not seventeen, as she had claimed), invited her to move in with his family.

When asked why he had done that, he said, "It wasn't because I loved her and wanted to marry her later. It was just the right thing to do, that's all. I knew right from wrong, and I needed to take care of her." Nonetheless, he is still not certain what that entails and how much he should be involved.

Some guys are proud that they've fathered a child. Max was like that. He was two years older than his girl-friend, who was fourteen at the time of her pregnancy.

ASK DR. JAN, PSYCHOLOGIST

First name: Jovonna

Question:

What do you do if you become pregnant and don't want your parents to know and the guy you're pregnant by doesn't want you anymore? Can I handle raising the baby myself?

Answer:

While it is certainly possible that you could handle raising the baby by yourself, it will be an extremely difficult and challenging task. Even with a supportive family and father, being a teen parent is tough. You should seek the advice of a health professional to ensure that you and the baby are in good health and to explore your options. If you decide to have the baby on your own, it will be important for you to know what services are available in your community. Consider contacting a social worker or counselor at your school to find out about available teen parent support and educational services. You can also contact your local social services department to find out what it offers.

Even though it may be very challenging, you may want to reconsider telling your parents. Chances are they are going to find out eventually as your pregnancy continues and of course once you give birth and have your baby. If you are determined to raise your child, you will really benefit from your parents' help and support during the challenging times ahead.

Ask a Question

Do you have a question that you would like answered? E-mail your question to Dr. Jan at drjan@rosenpub.com. If your question is selected, it will appear on the Teen Health & Wellness Web site in "Dr. Jan's Corner."

If you have an urgent question on a health or wellness issue, we strongly encourage you to call a hotline to speak to a qualified professional or speak to a trusted adult, such as a parent, teacher, or guidance counselor. You can find hotlines listed in the For More Information section of this book, or at www.teenhealthandwellness.com/static/hotlines.

Max thought it was great that she was pregnant. He had no concept of what parenthood required; his contribution was to buy diapers for the baby once every week.

Some guys may be angry. The anger may be focused on the girl who is carrying their baby or on the government for making him support a child he never wanted.

Hank was a high school sophomore when his girlfriend got pregnant. Neither cared enough about the other to marry, but Hank still wanted to be involved in their baby's welfare. During his senior year, he rearranged his class schedule so that he could care for the baby while his former girlfriend went to classes. After graduation, she gave him custody of their child. Hank, even with good intent, just couldn't manage single parenthood and work. His mother ended up raising the baby, and Hank grew increasingly depressed at his early failure to be a good father.

Some guys feel no responsibility toward the child or the child's mother. They don't think of them as "their problem." Ted said, "I gave Lisa some money for an abortion, but she didn't get one. I can't help that. I told her I didn't want to be involved; I didn't want that kid. My part is finished; I don't intend to spend the rest of my life supporting a kid I didn't want in the first place. She wanted it; let her raise it."

Although Ted claimed that he felt no responsibility toward the baby or the mother, he was so angry that it was not hard to pick up on his ambivalence. It was several months before he could admit his own anger and tie it into his need to see himself as a good person, one who does not turn his back on others. Ted sent money to Lisa for child support, although he still wrestled with the role of "father."

Very few guys are enthusiastic about their young girl-friend's pregnancy, especially when they have no plan to marry. However, some guys are still interested and committed, despite their initial shock and anger. Some girls and their boyfriends do their weekly grocery shopping together, although the girl still lives with her parents and raises the baby with their support. The men are interested in their children and remain involved, even though their own relationship with the baby's mother appears shaky.

Single parenthood does not have to be the end of the world. It is hard—after all, without a partner you have to shoulder more responsibilities. You have twice the chores and only half the support. But with community and family help, single parenthood can be made easier.

During the past few decades, the courts have attempted to overturn the 1973 Supreme Court ruling legalizing abortion (known as *Roe* v. *Wade*) or to severely restrict its application, state by state. Despite the ongoing controversy, however, abortion is still legal.

President Bill Clinton favored a woman's right to choose, so significant changes regarding abortion occurred in the 1990s. The pro-life movement gained considerable momentum during George W. Bush's presidency in 2001, its goal being to persuade the Supreme Court to outlaw abortion. To that end, militants marched on abortion clinics, harassing both the women who sought abortions and the doctors who performed the procedure. Over the following years, pro-life advocates have succeeded in curtailing many of the rights *Roe* v. *Wade* originally ensured.

In December 1992, a federally funded clinic would not have been able to give teenagers abortion information or even a referral to an agency that would offer the information. In 1993, Clinton removed the gag order on providing abortion information and referral at clinics that receive government funds. However, Bush reinstituted the order in 2001. Soon after President Barack Obama took office in

ABORTION: AN OPTION FOR NOT HAVING THE BABY

January 2009, he repealed the policy. Women now have more options than they did in the past. Nevertheless, they need to remember two things. First, controversy rages on both sides of the abortion issue; since doctors David Gunn (in 1993), John Britton (in 1994), Barnett Slepian (in 1998), and George Tiller (in 2009) were shot and killed for performing abortions, many people have been hesitant to take their place. For young pregnant women, that means it may be harder to get the service they desire. Second, many states now restrict abortion. A young woman may be required to tell her parents (or partner) before she can seek an abortion, and she may be required to wait twenty-four hours before the procedure can be done. People should not let these restrictions deter them if this is the option they choose. If they happen to live in such a state, they can drive to a state that does not have these restrictions. They can also seek the court's permission to have the abortion without informing their parents (usually granted in cases of abusive relationships). Otherwise, they can inform their parents. Delaying solves nothing; it merely removes options.

Informing an individual's parents need not mean the end of the world. Often, they do not react as badly as the person fears. Still, in the event that the young woman is seriously upset about their possible reactions, she can ask employees at a family planning clinic to help her break the news to them. Most parents would rather know the situation (and thus support their daughter) than leave such an important decision in her hands alone.

A young woman, Sara, came to see Carolyn Simpson's colleague after being raped by her stepfather and having a subsequent abortion. Philosophically, Sara had been dead set against abortion, but then she was not expecting the father of her stepbrothers to become the father of her baby. One evening when she was at home alone, her stepfather raped her. When Sara later discovered she was pregnant, she was so overwhelmed with disgust that she scheduled an immediate abortion. She never told her family.

Sara told her counselor, "I never thought I'd have an abortion. I never meant to, and I don't feel so great about what I did. I try to think of it simply as my stepfather's kid. It wasn't right, what he did to me. That baby wasn't conceived in love or even in a moment of lust. It wasn't my choice. Why should I have had to live with that the rest of my life?"

Another woman Simpson met during her work as a clinical social worker, counselor, and teacher described why she had an abortion. Mary was seventeen when her first child was born. A family crisis had been brewing for some time, and Mary had attempted to deal with it by risking a pregnancy with her boyfriend. Mary chose not to marry her boyfriend. She remained at home with her parents (who were supportive but embarrassed by the circumstances), and she ultimately delivered a little girl she named Cindy. Her parents helped with child care, and Mary returned to high school to get her diploma.

A year after Cindy was born, Mary became pregnant again. This time she could not bear to tell her parents or even her boyfriend. She went alone to a clinic and had the abortion. When Simpson talked with Mary—several months after the abortion—she was struck by Mary's unacknowledged guilt. Mary kept saying, "It was no big deal." In fact, she probably said that twelve times in the space of an hour. When Simpson asked what she meant, Mary finally blurted out, "I knew I couldn't have another baby so soon. Not in those circumstances. I didn't think of it as a baby or anything. The abortion hurt a little, but that wasn't any big deal. When I got home, I picked up Cindy to change her. I looked at her, and I kept seeing this other baby that might have been. That was the only time I felt the immensity of what I had done. I really haven't thought about it much since."

The above stories—both true, but disguised to protect the identities of the individuals, as are all Simpson's stories recounted in this book—show that there are reasons for abortion other than simply backing up failed condoms or skipped pills. Sometimes there are good reasons for an abortion, and you should not have to feel condemned by a society that cannot come to a consensus on the subject. One thing you must realize about abortion, however, is that it's an option only if it is done early enough. First you have to figure out how far along your pregnancy is and whether the procedure can be done safely.

To determine just how pregnant you are, go back to your calendar (you should always keep track of your menstrual cycle) and find out when you last had your period. Pinpoint the first day of that period and count it as day 1.

1. Why do you feel unable to carry this child?

2. Have you talked this over with your boyfriend?

3. Do you know a reputable clinic or doctor to perform the abortion?

4. Do you have the money?

5. Do you have a support person to go through the experience with you?

6. Are you opting for abortion to please someone else or out of fear?

7. Can you live with this decision the rest of your life?

8. Do you know who to turn to with regret or guilt?

CONSIDERING ABORTION

Then count the weeks until you arrive at today's date. For example, if your last period began on June 1 and today's date is August 31, you are thirteen weeks pregnant. (It may not seem to make sense because you probably were not pregnant on day 1 of your period, but that is how doctors figure it out, and those are the dates the doctor will be looking at in considering an abortion.)

Unfortunately for many teenagers, denial of the obvious symptoms or sheer ignorance hinders the chances for a safe abortion. The ideal time for an abortion is between seven and twelve weeks of pregnancy. The type done at this point is called a vacuum aspiration abortion (also called suction aspiration), and it takes between five and fifteen minutes to perform. For a woman who is less than twelve weeks pregnant, this type of abortion can be done in a clinic relatively easily and safely.

ABORTION CHOICES

There are several methods of abortion. When a woman chooses a procedure to end her pregnancy, it is called induced abortion. According to the American Congress of Obstetricians and Gynecologists (ACOG), the majority of abortions are performed in the first twelve weeks of a woman's pregnancy. A woman can choose to end a pregnancy by having a medical abortion (also called a chemical abortion) or a surgical abortion. In a medical abortion, the woman takes medicine, which causes the abortion. Most physicians do not recommend that a woman have a medical abortion after nine weeks of pregnancy. (The first trimester of a pregnancy is about five to twelve weeks.) Surgical abortions are procedures where the lining of the womb is removed. There are two types of surgical abortions: manual vacuum aspiration (MVA) and dilation and evacuation (D & E). Both surgical methods use suction to draw the tissue out of the womb. The MVA procedure can be performed within the first twelve weeks of a pregnancy. The D & E method can be performed after the first month but before the end of the thirteenth week of pregnancy. (The second trimester is at about thirteen to twenty-four weeks.) The later in the woman's pregnancy that a procedure is done, the more complicated the procedure becomes and the higher the risk is to the woman's health.

Between twelve and sixteen weeks of pregnancy, the dilation and curettage (D & C) abortion is performed. General anesthesia is administered, and the doctor may take between twelve and twenty minutes to dilate the cervix and scrape and suction out the contents of the uterus. Needless to say, it is a more costly and uncomfortable procedure.

A saline abortion is done up to twenty-four weeks of pregnancy. Liquid is introduced into the woman's body to start the contractions of labor. This procedure is done in the hospital and involves a two- to three-day stay. It is far more costly, and it is painful. It is also far more traumatic because the fetus looks more like a baby.

After twenty-four weeks of pregnancy, the fetus is considered viable and an abortion will not be performed except in a medical emergency. At this stage, it would more than likely be a live birth.

The abortion pill, called RU-486 (mifepristone), is available in the United States from doctors and family planning clinics. It is used in chemical/medical abortions. A chemical abortion is a complicated process and more time consuming than a surgical abortion. The financial cost of the RU-486 abortion is similar to that of a surgical abortion.

Here's how it works: a woman who is no more than forty-nine days pregnant takes three 200-milligram tablets of mifepristone at her doctor's office. The drug causes the fetus to die. The fetus dies when the pill stops the woman's body from providing blood and nutrition to the uterine wall, which nourishes the fetus. Two days later, the woman makes a second visit to her doctor's office and takes two tablets of another medication called misoprostol, a prostaglandin. This drug causes the uterus to contract until it expels the fetus. The woman remains under observation for several hours. However, not all women will abort in that time period. Usually, the fetus is expelled within fourteen days of taking the mifepristone. The woman makes a third visit to the doctor to verify (usually by exam or ultrasound) that the fetus was completely expelled.

The RU-486 abortion has some disadvantages of which you should be aware. Side effects associated with the abortion pill are heavy bleeding, nausea, vomiting, and severe uterine cramping. Also, you cannot know where or when you will expel the fetus. Moreover, if your body does not expel the fetus, you will need to undergo a surgical abortion.

Although it is not ideal for teenagers to seek abortions as a solution to unplanned pregnancies, for some, it is simply the lesser of two evils. Teenagers should be prepared for deceptive practices that have been found in some clinics.

If you are thinking about having an abortion, you should know that there are two very different types of family planning clinics. Some clinics that advertise free pregnancy testing are actually antiabortion organizations that first show you a graphic film of an abortion. The film usually depicts a late-stage procedure with accompanying trauma to the fetus, which looks very much like an infant. It is misleading because first-trimester abortions performed before twelve weeks of pregnancy do not look like that. The film is designed to make you change your mind and continue the pregnancy. Antiabortion people are probably not interested in your reasons for having an abortion. They have their own agenda, which is to deter women from having abortions.

At the other kind of family planning clinic, counselors explain the procedures of abortion and detail the alternatives. You can explore your feelings

A manager at a family planning clinic waits for a teen client who is seeking an abortion to complete the clinic's paperwork. Do not allow clinic employees to mislead you or take away your right to choose whether to have the baby or have an abortion.

about the options. It is not their intent to sway your way of thinking, whatever that may be. They may show you a film, but it will probably be of an early abortion and will be sensitively done.

How do you tell these clinics apart before the damage is done? First, ask others who may have gone to one of them. If that is not possible, choose a clinic but leave at the first indication that the counselor wants to sell you on a certain solution. If you are subjected to a film whose graphic content horrifies you, leave. As mentioned earlier, a first-trimester abortion does not involve delivery of a baby-like fetus. All that you see is blood and tissue.

Many family planning clinics that do not offer abortions still provide services to a woman who has undergone an abortion elsewhere. Even if a clinic does not provide abortions, it may offer follow-up support, such as a twelve-step recovery program, to women who have had abortions. These recovery programs help women deal with the guilt and other powerful emotions that may arise after having an abortion.

AFTER MAKING YOUR DECISION

Just because you are young, vulnerable, and asking for assistance should not mean that you have to give up your ability to choose. It is still a decision that is entirely up to you. Remember, no one has the right to force you to have the baby or, for that matter, have the abortion—not your counselor, your parents, your doctor, or your boyfriend.

It is hard to avoid having strong emotions about abortion, not only because society is in an uproar about a woman's right to abortion, but because people, as

A clinic counselor answers a young woman's questions about abortion procedures and the emotional
and physical effects.

fallible human beings, are likely to make mistakes and
blame themselves for them.

You will probably be angry about getting into the
predicament in the first place. In addition, you will be
upset about having to go through this experience when
your boyfriend—who played a part in the making of the
baby—has no immediate sense of the trauma. You may

think that he has it easy. It is maddening to think back on that moment in time when your boyfriend assured you he'd be there forever and now realize that you're the one having an abortion.

You may also feel ashamed and guilty for 1) getting pregnant, and 2) having an abortion. If you're feeling unsure of your decision, it's important to talk it over with a concerned adult, preferably your parents or a counselor who is sympathetic.

At some family planning organizations and support groups, clinic counselors try to explore all possibilities, examining their client's values to determine whether abortion is a decision the client will be able to look back on later without regret. Abortion is hard enough. Don't punish yourself further for having chosen that course.

Guilt comes out in strange ways. Teddy was a junior in high school when she became pregnant. She had been a drug user and had finally come to grips with her addiction. When she had found her way out of the dark and was working on graduating and staying clean, she discovered she was pregnant. She was not able to care for a baby. She talked with her school guidance counselor and then went through with an uncomplicated abortion. She seemed to handle the aftermath well, except for one matter: she kept having bad dreams.

"I dreamed once that I had the baby and was giving it a bath," she explained. "I left the room for a second—just one second—to get a towel. When I came back, the baby was face down in the tub. Dead. I woke up in a panic, and I remembered that I had killed my baby. It took a while before I realized I hadn't exactly killed it. Not that way."

It is not unusual to have such dreams. What happened was that what Teddy had not worked through during the daytime got into her dreams at night. Her mind was still trying to work the whole situation out during sleep. If you have dreams that are repetitive or scary, counseling may help you resolve your difficulty. Once the problem is recognized and conquered, the bad dreams should stop.

Even if abortion is the right choice, guilt can still plague you. Ellen is a professor at a prestigious college in Maine. Ten years earlier, while still in high school, she had become pregnant by her boyfriend, Harry. Ellen had planned to go to college the following year. Furthermore, she was not sure she and Harry could be mates for life. She just wasn't ready for that kind of relationship.

She and Harry drove to another city for the abortion. Ellen felt that she was making the right decision, but because of her strong religious background, she also believed what she was doing was wrong.

She had the abortion, and Harry took her home. Ellen never told her family. She refused to let Harry talk about his own feelings; she just wanted to pretend the whole thing had never happened. Later, she kept having bad dreams. She considered going to confession, but her priest had very strong feelings about abortion, and she believed he would merely compound her anguish by condemning her action. Not feeling pardoned but still feeling guilty, Ellen dropped out of the church. Every time she saw Harry, she remembered the abortion, and in some strange way she began to blame him for the whole thing. They eventually broke up, but they remained friends.

What brought Ellen into the hospital where Carolyn Simpson worked was the birth of Harry's first child, very near the ten-year anniversary of her abortion. When Simpson saw Ellen, she had tried to overdose on sleeping pills. Her parents had no idea what torment Ellen was going through.

During treatment, in addition to listening as Ellen unloaded her guilt and anger, Simpson found a sympathetic priest who did not know Ellen. Simpson left them in her office so that Ellen could make a formal confession after all those years, knowing that she would never have to see this priest again. Simpson can't say that the confession alleviated all of Ellen's guilt, but it did help her start talking about the abortion. She was able to realize that not all of society condemned her and that God could forgive her. Gradually she came to see that she had made the right decision at the age of eighteen, even though it was one that she was not particularly proud of.

Aside from feeling guilty, you may also be nervous about having an abortion when so many people are making a public issue out of it. Not all clinics that perform abortions have picketers outside, but some draw angry crowds of both pro-life and pro-choice advocates. Federal court rulings have made it illegal for picketers to bully or prevent you from entering the clinic, but those rulings do nothing to keep them from yelling at you.

You may not be happy with what you're about to do (even if you know it's the right choice for you), so having people scream at you can be unnerving. It's easy to say, "Don't listen to the protesters," or "Ignore the signs they carry"; but that is not that easy to do. For this reason, take along a support person and ask the clinic doctors and nurses to keep an eye out for your arrival. Sometimes all the media attention will make you angry rather than scared. Besides, that is not so strange; these people are taking something very personal and making it into a public spectacle.

Shrouding the abortion in secrecy (as many teens feel they must do) only complicates the adjustment afterward. When you can't talk about what you've been through, you have no way to unburden your guilt, anger, or sadness. You may end up feeling like a criminal, bottling up your emotions and denying that anything significant happened. Sometimes women who have had abortions and no supportive counseling later turn against others who had the same procedure. Some of the most adamant antiabortion people are those who once had abortions themselves.

Some young women are simply frightened of abortion. If you are one of them, it's important for your own peace of mind to obtain as much information as possible about the available procedures. A good family planning clinic can help you with the specifics. A good resource for straightforward information is *Our Bodies, Ourselves: A New Edition for a New Era* (2005). Most people are afraid of things they don't fully understand. It's OK to be scared.

Simpson spoke with a young woman who had seen one of the abortion "scare" films. Although not considering abortion for herself, she was further frightened about childbirth. "I had not really thought about having the kid," she said. "But that film made me realize that I was going to have to go through something similar whether I wanted an abortion or a baby. It was scary."

Another reaction common to people who have had abortions is denial, acting as if the whole experience was "no big deal." Ironically, it seems as if the women have no particular feelings at all. If you find yourself not able to conjure up a single emotion, dig a little deeper beneath the apathy. Feelings are there, but you may have to search for them. Just because you *think* you don't feel anything about the abortion does not mean that you don't. Some people are able to do something called compartmentalizing the pain. It is as though they take out the pain and put it in a special drawer and then close the drawer, blocking out the pain. It works for a while, but usually people who block out pain block out their "good" feelings as well.

More than likely, you will have a mixture of emotions. Initially, you may feel relieved that "the problem has gone away." Later you become angry at the world because this situation or experience happened to you. Neither one of those feelings is wrong. You are not a bad person because you chose to have an abortion. Abortion is just one alternative that must be examined carefully if you find yourself unexpectedly pregnant. You must feel that it is right for you. In Simpson's practice, she had never met anyone who did not express some regret over an abortion. Not that they would make any other decision. In most cases, given the same circumstances, they would again elect to have the abortion. They simply realize that a loss is a loss. It hurts.

THE GUY'S VIEWPOINT

What about the guy in all this? What about the child's father's wishes?

You cannot force your girlfriend to have the baby if she opts for an abortion. Because it is her body, the decision is ultimately hers to make. However, the developing fetus is a part of you, and you may feel it is wrong to end the pregnancy.

Share your feelings with your girlfriend. Discuss other options, such as adoption. You could elect to raise the baby yourself if your girlfriend agrees to terminate her rights.

No matter what, however, you cannot force her to have the child. If she is determined to have an abortion, talk to her about her feelings. Perhaps she only needs to hear that you will stick this out with her. On the other hand, maybe you're being unrealistic; give her a chance to explain her position.

Some guys want to be supportive of their girlfriend and to go to the clinic with her for the abortion. Make sure your girlfriend wants you to be there. Offer your support, but be aware that she may prefer to go alone.

ASK DR. JAN, PSYCHOLOGIST

First name: Brandon

Question:
My boyfriend just got me pregnant. Now he has left me to have it on my own. I think I should get an abortion. How do I figure out my options and whether abortion is the right decision for me?

Answer:
The first thing you want to do is research what resources are available in your community. In many states, there are women's health clinics (or teen health clinics) that provide services for teens, including health professionals that you can talk to who will educate you about your options and help you make an informed decision. You may also want to contact your local public health department and ask what services they have available.

Another option is to confide in a parent. If that's not possible, perhaps there's a trusted adult at your school or in your community that you could confide in. Maybe they can help you locate resources and perhaps go with you to keep you company.

This is a very tough decision in your young life. It is important that you have as much information and support as possible to help you make the right decision for you.

Ask a Question
Do you have a question that you would like answered? E-mail your question to Dr. Jan at drjan@rosenpub.com. If your question is selected, it will appear on the Teen Health & Wellness Web site in "Dr. Jan's Corner."

If you have an urgent question on a health or wellness issue, we strongly encourage you to call a hotline to speak to a qualified professional or speak to a trusted adult, such as a parent, teacher, or guidance counselor. You can find hotlines listed in the For More Information section of this book, or at www. teenhealthandwellness.com/static/hotlines.

You may not be able to hold her hand through the procedure, but you can be with her while she is waiting (and often the waiting is worse than the procedure). You can also be there with her when she's recovering.

Let her talk. She may be mad, or she may be scared and want comfort. Be prepared for anything, and don't take what she says personally. Even in labor, women often make outrageous comments to their partners. It is only because they're hurting and don't always realize what comes out of their mouths. Your girlfriend is hurting both emotionally and physically. Understand that she may say things that she doesn't really mean. If you are angry, too, or upset and sad, share your feelings later when you think she can handle them.

Some guys feel nothing but horror over a girlfriend's pregnancy. All they want to do is get as far away as possible from the situation. So they run, physically or emotionally—an option not available to the woman who is carrying the child.

Overall, it is more difficult for a guy to feel that initial bonding with the unborn child because his body is not undergoing the physical changes. Some young men grieve over the loss of the child, but at this point—in the teen years—they are seldom sufficiently invested in either the girlfriend or the pregnancy to grieve for what might have been. For some young men who realize that they have years ahead of them in which to start a family, suggesting an abortion to their girlfriend may not seem to be such horrible advice to give.

FINISHING HIGH SCHOOL

This chapter delves into how a pregnancy affects the other parts of a teen's life. One of the biggest traps for pregnant teens is choosing not to complete their schooling. True, not everyone is cut out for college, and for that matter, not everyone needs a college degree. A high school diploma is different, though. The unfortunate thing that often happens when a teenager becomes pregnant is that she drops out of school. Or her boyfriend, realizing that he will need to support a child, drops out to take on an additional job.

Struggling to find ways to cover the bills is a very unpleasant way to live. Without a high school diploma, you subject yourself to minimum-wage jobs. Money will be a constant concern, as if the new problems of parenthood will not be troubling enough. However you do it, try to complete high school. As an adult who herself has seen financially troubling times, according to Simpson, getting a good job and feeling good about yourself because you can support your family are two of the most important goals you can have in your life.

Certainly, it's hard to stay in school. First of all, you are probably too embarrassed to attend classes right through your pregnancy. Bonnie told Simpson about her embarrassment. When she was first pregnant, Bonnie still rode the bus to school, hoping to go on with her education as if nothing had changed. The problem was that she was different now, and one of the biggest lessons learned in adolescence is that no one wants to be different. Bonnie was not only married, she was very noticeably pregnant. Some kids laughed behind her back because she looked different trying to squeeze herself into a seat. Some may have giggled because they were uncomfortable with the idea of Bonnie's sexuality. That can make a person nervous if he or she is embarrassed about the whole idea of sex. But whatever the reasons for other people's behavior, it makes it hard to parade your body around the schoolyard, which is exactly what Bonnie felt she was doing. Bonnie finally dropped out of school to have the baby. Ten years later, she went back to join a program to earn her high school diploma.

"I can start feeling good about myself," she said. "I always believed I wasn't as good as anyone else because I hadn't finished high school."

Aside from looking different, you will probably be acting different, too. Morning sickness and school never mix well. Who wants to keep running back and forth to the restroom all day?

Sometimes it is not even a matter of embarrassment about your appearance. When a woman is pregnant, it is normal for her to be consumed with what is going on inside her. She fantasizes about the unborn child, she names it, she wonders what it will be like to cuddle this new life wriggling around inside. Much of her energy is spent just thinking about the baby. The same is true of a teenager. She is preoccupied with the "miracle of life" unfolding inside her. Will she have a baby shower? Will she do OK in labor and delivery? Will she be a good mother? Will her baby love her? What will it look like? With all this wondering and figuring, it's not hard to see that little room is left for studying.

Some girls aspire to nothing beyond motherhood. "I'm not the type of girl who wants a career," Nicole said. "I'm going to stay home and take care of my family, so what does it matter if I drop out of school a little early?"

The drawback of dropping out of school is that you limit your chances for the future by deciding at age fifteen or sixteen that you will never want a career. What if your boyfriend fails to come through with the money? What if your soon-to-be husband discovers that he hates being married and wants a divorce? What if your parents tell you you're on your own now? Whatever your ideas are about welfare assistance, when it comes down to it, it is never enough. With no money and no job prospects (beyond those that will pay you only the bare minimum wages), you will be trapped in that house, responsible for your young children, and eventually you'll become resentful of your loss of a meaningful life.

There have been times when Simpson stayed home to raise her three children. The difference for her—in the past, as a career woman—was that she knew she had the means by which to secure a well-paying job if she needed it. Simpson always knew she could take care of herself, and she thought that was important in feeling good about oneself.

These teen mothers in Minnesota drop their children off at a day care program at their high school. The program enables the young mothers to attend classes so that they can finish high school and graduate.

If you are anything like Simpson was thirty years ago, you're probably reading this chapter with about as much enthusiasm as you would feel preparing for midterms. When Simpson was in college, all she wanted to do was get married; she was afraid the opportunity would pass her by and she'd never get another. She assumed she could interrupt her college career, get married, and work at any job to help keep her husband in school. Then she and her husband would raise a family, and eventually she would get around to finishing college—although she didn't know what she intended to do with the children in the meantime.

Fortunately for her, her father talked Simpson out of it. He predicted that she would never finish her education if she turned her back on it right then. Simpson thought at the time that her father was condemning her to the single life forever because by the time she finished school she'd be too old to enkindle anyone's interest in marriage.

When she was in graduate school (and was also married), Simpson realized what a hard task she had set for herself. Looking back at her plan to abandon school for marriage, she realized that she probably never would have made her way back into the system. The longer you're out, the harder it is.

Occasionally (and this was true for some of the women mentioned in this book) the girl has already given up on school and dropped out. Then she may become pregnant. Terry, at fourteen, had become fed up with school. Like so many other teenagers, she did not abruptly decide to quit; it happened gradually. She missed a few days of school, attended on others, and then skipped a week or so. The overburdened guidance department gave up tracking down a teenager who couldn't make up her mind to remain a student. Terry admitted that she was just "out of it" and no one came after her to make her return to school.

1. If you dropped out of school, how are you planning to support yourself for the rest of your life?
2. If you're married, what will you do for money should your husband die or desert you?
3. If you think you might one day return to school, how will you manage it (child care, cost, time)?
4. What type of job or career would you like to hold if money were no obstacle?
5. What do you see yourself doing five or ten years down the road?

GIVING UP YOUR EDUCATION

It is impossible to know exactly why teens drop out of school. Obviously Terry and girls like her had found little academic success in the past. For a teenager already having academic difficulties, pregnancy is often the best reason (in her eyes) to drop out of school. "Why bother now?" she seems to say.

PROGRAMS FOR CONTINUING YOUR EDUCATION

Taking regular classes is not the only way to get an education or a diploma. Several special programs are in operation to help the pregnant teenager fulfill her school obligations and raise her child as well. Some places have mentor programs whereby an older teen or adult is

Teen moms from high schools in central Illinois attend an extension class at a community college to learn about using a checkbook and other real-world lessons on financial matters. Many schools offer learning opportunities for teen mothers.

paired with a newly pregnant teenager. This older person helps the younger one navigate the difficulties in getting assistance and may even act as a tutor.

Other schools encourage the girl to graduate by enrolling her in adult education classes so that she no longer has to attend school with people her own age who might make her feel uncomfortable.

Special programs linked with the school (or adult education) serve as an alternative to regular classes. In one program Simpson visited, the girls, most of whom had children and could bring them to day care in the same building, attended classes with other teens in similar circumstances. Because the building was not on school grounds, the girls did not feel conspicuous for attending something different. It was simply another program to fulfill unique needs. The girls learned at their own pace, received a great deal of individual attention, and more important, had the opportunity to discuss in a class setting with professionals what was happening in their lives now that they had children or were pregnant. Other school programs blend students into the main-stream of regular classes. The teenagers in one of these programs did not feel awkward around the other non-pregnant students. Babysitters at the parenting center, located right on campus, looked after their babies, and the only difference between these girls and their peers was that they arrived and departed the school with infants. Consequently, they were able to attend classes and finish their high school education. The staff of this innovative program supported the girls and gave them something more to aspire to than a minimum-wage job and child care hassles.

Some of these programs encourage teen fathers to participate as well. Guys, especially ones who decide to help support their new family, often feel stretched thin by the demands of work, homework, and thoughts of impending fatherhood. They have little energy left to concentrate on studies, perhaps fearing they may have to give up their aspirations to further their educa-tion. Programs such as the one mentioned earlier can offer supportive counseling to the anxious teen father. These programs are being established all over the country because of the large number of pregnant teenagers. Apparently lawmakers have decided that if they cannot prevent teenage pregnancies, they should do something to help the pregnant teen finish her schooling.

Even if you are embarrassed or uncomfortable about being pregnant and in school, you can search out alternatives to strike a balance between your needs for privacy and an education. Your diploma (and certainly college) is your opportunity to break out of the cycle.

CHAPTER 6

KEEPING YOUR FRIENDS

Your relationship with your best friend can change for many reasons over the years: One of you marries, one moves away, one has a baby. Despite the fact that babies are supposed to be bundles of joy, it's hard to believe they can alter your friendships as much as they do.

When you're pregnant, you may find it hard to relate to your friends who are not married or pregnant. You have different interests, and it will take much effort to understand one another's lives right now.

Aside from the glow of accomplishment, you may feel regret. You can't party anymore—not if you're concerned about your baby's well-being. Drugs, alcohol, and babies don't mix. If you want a healthy baby, you have to stay away from those things and the friends who still pursue them.

Chandra told Simpson that her best friend was angry with her, now that she had a baby. Simpson asked if it was because Chandra had something she didn't have, but Chandra thought it was because her friend didn't like to party without her. She felt that Chandra had deserted her.

Right after the birth, Chandra was so excited about the baby that she didn't mind staying home night after night. Soon, though, the novelty of looking after a baby wore off, and Chandra grew resentful of her best friend's freedom.

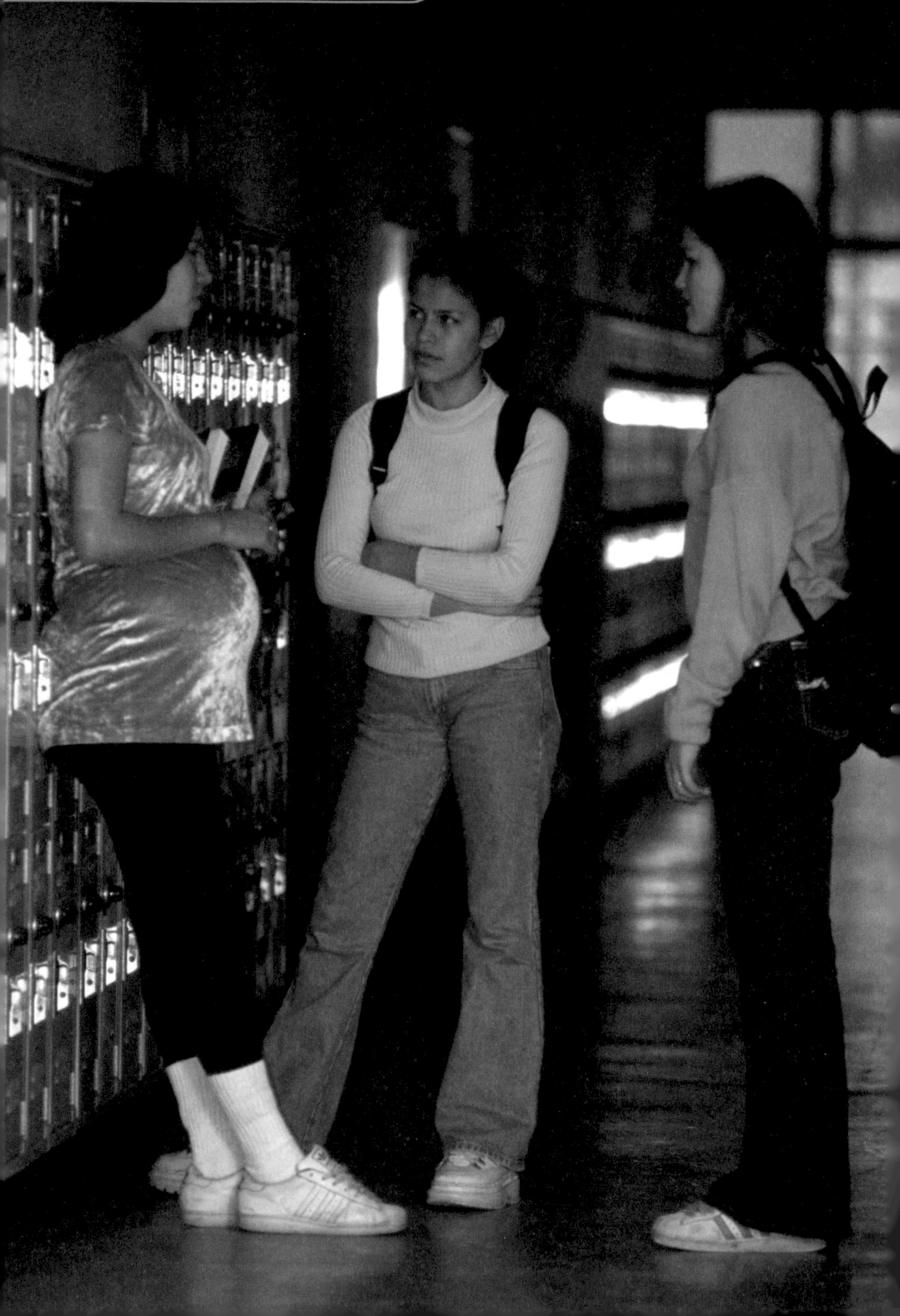

Ironically, the best friend who thought Chandra was crazy for giving up her freedom became pregnant shortly after Chandra's baby turned one month old. Now Chandra is once again looking forward to having things in common with her best friend.

It is frustrating for everyone concerned when someone in your group of friends becomes pregnant. The other girls may grow bored hearing about your pregnancy once the newness wears off, and you probably tire of hearing about events in which you can no longer participate. Differences sometimes complicate relationships, particularly if you and your friends cannot talk about the subject and find some middle ground.

Some years ago, Simpson ran a group for inpatients at the hospital where she worked. One girl who had a baby thought the world existed just to ponder her postpartum depression. Finally, a woman in the group shouted, "If you say one more word about your baby or your hard life, I'm going to throw up. I've heard enough to last me a lifetime."

To a degree, you may find yourself in the same boat with your friends, who are not interested in hearing about your baby because they are not having a baby.

If drugs and alcohol are part of your friendships, you need to find other friends or ask your friends to avoid their vices around you. In the first three months of

A pregnant teen talks with her friends between classes at their high school. It is a challenge to maintain your friendships when you are a mother-to-be, but don't stop making the effort, especially when those friendships are a positive influence.

pregnancy, drugs—even some prescription drugs—can damage development of the fetus. Remember, whatever you, the mother, ingest crosses the placental barrier, and the baby ingests it, too. Drinking beer and wine that can supposedly relax you can retard the baby's growth and in severe cases can cause the baby's death. There is no time when a pregnant woman can safely drink alcohol. In the end, your friends may not appreciate your new circumstances and your wanting them to change their habits. Even drinking more than one cup of coffee per day, according to studies reported by the March of Dimes, can contribute to a miscarriage.

Some girls have told Simpson that at least one friend has tried to maintain the old ties. They say that they both make extra efforts to keep the friendship going, but they add, "It's not the same, though."

So how do you cope with the havoc your pregnancy wreaks on your friendships? First of all, you have to accept that your friends will not always change just because you did, and they probably won't marvel at your new situation if it's nothing they want at this time. You can keep these people in your life, but as the pregnancy progresses, they are likely to take a backseat to other acquaintances. You might consider a whole new set of friends who reinforce a positive image and have more in common with you.

You may be asking, "Well, where do I find these people?" It's not difficult. There are special classes and support groups for pregnant teenagers who are still in school. Some are associated with the school, and others

1. How important are your current friends?
2. What do you have in common with them?
3. Do you have any other friends in similar circumstances?
4. Who do you have for company besides your immediate family?
5. Do your friends use drugs or alcohol? Do you? Can you stop?

GIVING UP YOUR FRIENDS

are associated with the YWCA. You should be able to find others who have either been where you are now or are going through it, too. Called peer support groups, they are forming all over the country to serve the needs of pregnant teens. It's just a matter of asking where they are in your community.

Then, too, when you take Lamaze classes, you will meet an assortment of people preparing for birth. These childbirth classes are a great way to learn about delivery and pregnancy and to make friends. When Simpson took the classes, the participants were all as interested in hearing about each other's aches and pains as they were in the deliveries. She said she felt she had a whole group of people cheering her on as she got through the stages of pregnancy.

Incidentally, in taking Lamaze classes you don't necessarily commit yourself to an unmedicated childbirth. The classes merely help you understand the process. You can still ask for medication for your delivery.

Teen parents work on Lamaze techniques in a birthing class. In many Lamaze classes, parents learn about the stages and signs of labor, birth, and recovery, and basic information about baby care.

Finally, don't lose sight of the fact that you have a life beyond that of being a mother. You will get tired of tying yourself down to your baby. Cultivate other interests by hanging onto some of your old friends and letting them keep you involved in the world at large. You may not feel as close to them as you once did, but you don't have to go to the other extreme: shutting them out of your life.

You may be unsure about how you will be able to hang onto your old friends after your baby arrives. Two ways to help you keep your friends are the following:

- Involve an old friend in your new life. Invite her to spend an afternoon at your place while the baby naps. That way the two of you can have time together.
- Schedule time away from the baby so that you can participate in your old friend's world. Talk about your differences if misunderstandings develop. Remind her that she's still important to you.

Your life should not come to a standstill simply because you've become a mother. Keep involved and challenged so that you feel alive and important. Your baby will eventually grow up and leave your home. What you have done with your life up to that point will sustain you once the kids have left the nest.

THE GUY'S VIEWPOINT

Young men will face some of the same problems, depending on how involved they are with their girlfriends or wives. They, too, may see less and less of their old friends. Some guys can adapt better to these changes than others. Some will be angry that their new responsibilities require them to give up some of their pastimes. They may think they have given up enough.

Those of you who spend less time with your buddies may find yourself resentful, not only because you've had to change, but also because your girlfriend may not be able to fill the gap left by these friends. She may be preoccupied with the coming baby, which leaves you feeling even more jealous and deserted.

ASK DR. JAN, PSYCHOLOGIST

First name: Briana

Question:
Do I need to change my lifestyle now that I'm pregnant? Because I'm pregnant, will my friends still want to do things with me, and will they respect me?

Answer:
Being pregnant results in profound lifestyle changes, especially for a teen. As an expectant mother, it is important to take good care of your own health and the health of your baby. This usually requires regular doctor visits, eating a healthy diet, getting enough sleep, and abstinence from alcohol, tobacco, and other drugs.

There will also be changes to your school experience because of the increased challenges of pregnancy. Some school districts offer special programs for pregnant mothers that try to help them graduate high school, as pregnant teens have a high drop-out rate.

While your friends may still want to do things with you, being pregnant typically can limit the kind of activities you can engage in because of your new responsibilities, physical limitations, and recreational restrictions. That's why pregnant teens often have difficulty maintaining their social relationships during pregnancy and even more so after the baby is born.

If your friends are true friends, they will continue to respect you. What's important is that you respect yourself. You have a significant challenge in your life and you are trying to do what you think is best. That takes courage. Focusing on your health and the health of your child will help you stay on track. Try to identify trusted friends and adults in your life who can provide you with the emotional support that you will need.

Ask a Question

Do you have a question that you would like answered? E-mail your question to Dr. Jan at drjan@rosenpub.com. If your question is selected, it will appear on the Teen Health & Wellness Web site in "Dr. Jan's Corner."

If you have an urgent question on a health or wellness issue, we strongly encourage you to call a hotline to speak to a qualified professional or speak to a trusted adult, such as a parent, teacher, or guidance counselor. You can find hotlines listed in the For More Information section of this book, or at www.teenhealthandwellness.com/static/hotlines.

Try getting involved with other guys in the same circumstances or joining your girlfriend in Lamaze classes for the knowledge as well as the peer support. Cultivating new friends doesn't mean discarding all the old ones. Like your girlfriend, you still need contact with others who are involved in different pursuits.

Friendships usually change when a baby is coming; it's neither good nor bad that they change. Sometimes it helps to find a new circle of friends with similar interests while maintaining old friendships so that your life does not revolve only around your new family. Someday your old friends may have similar concerns, and they may look to you as the authority on the subject. You need not close doors to open new ones.

CHAPTER 7

The most difficult thing most pregnant teens had to do was to tell their family. Some girls went to great lengths to avoid having to tell them. This chapter recounts stories of families pulling together to give the teenager as much support as she or he needs to handle the challenges of teenage pregnancy. It also relates stories of just the opposite—families who turned their backs on the teenagers out of anger, shame, or ignorance.

YOUR RELATIONSHIP WITH YOUR PARENTS

The bond and rapport you had with your parents before your pregnancy will determine, to a large degree, the ease with which you tell them your news. In an already overburdened family, your parents may not react to the pregnancy beyond saying that they supposed you'd wind up pregnant. In other cases—even worse—your parents may not be in good enough emotional shape themselves to provide you with any kind of support or advice. One girl told Simpson that when she had confessed to her mother she was three months pregnant, her mother fell apart. Pamela ended up consoling her mother, telling her that things wouldn't be so bad and that she'd manage somehow. She went on to list the agencies that would probably help with finances, and eventually her mother calmed down. Years later, Pamela still recalled having to console her mother at a time in her life when she felt she was the one who needed support.

Some of you may be anxious that the news of your pregnancy will make your parents fly into a rage. Your parents may respond badly at first, but that doesn't mean they won't eventually stand by you. Sometimes it's not until the baby is born that the parents accept the situation.

Many of the girls interviewed said they thought their parents—especially their father—would "kill them." It is hard to believe that some parents react so unpleasantly, since they care so much for you. Perhaps they have a noble idea that they can give you the world and keep you safe from hardship at the same time. Discovering that you have created circumstances guaranteed to challenge your young life is no doubt more of a shock than they can initially absorb. Keep in mind, they may be just as mad at themselves for not protecting you as they are at you for getting into this predicament. You just have to get past everyone's initial hysteria.

Sometimes teenagers interpret their parents' strong reactions as shame and disgust. Then they take in those very emotions and end up feeling as guilty as they believe their parents consider them. A teenage pregnancy is indeed a family crisis, but it need not be the

Many teens believe the most difficult thing about their pregnancy was having to tell their parents. The type of relationship you had with your parents before you became pregnant will likely dictate the composure you will have when you inform them of your news.

family's downfall. Often, members pull together, despite their feelings of morality, for the very reason that they love you.

One girl told Simpson that she was too embarrassed to tell her parents she was pregnant. Lucy came from a religious family of an upper middle-class background. She had always been an excellent student, serious enough about her studies to go to an Ivy League college. During her senior year in high school, she became involved with a guy at school. He was good looking and charismatic, and before she knew it, she was sexually involved with him. She kept this aspect of their relationship from her parents, but after every date with Peter she felt horribly guilty. She would tiptoe past her parents' bedroom and pray they wouldn't wake up and talk with her. She was sure they would sense that she had sex with Peter, and she knew they considered sex before marriage as morally disgraceful and nothing their daughter would do.

When Lucy ended up pregnant, she was mostly ashamed because now they would know about her and Peter. She felt terrible about having let them down, not to mention that she was afraid of how it would affect the rest of her life.

Many girls said they were relieved when they finally told their parents. "It was all out in the open. I didn't have to lie awake at night anymore wondering how they would take the news," said Susan, age sixteen. "There was a lot of shouting and cursing at first, but we all survived it. Now my mother even takes me shopping for maternity clothes."

Allison was another girl who was afraid to tell her mother she thought she was pregnant. "There had been one family crisis after another that spring. I wasn't thrilled about dropping another bomb on her right then, but I told her anyway. You know what? She was just great. She told me I needed to get checked by our family doctor, and she even went with me for the appointment. I was actually relieved when the doctor gave me the verdict my mother already knew. She had to get married herself when she was pregnant, so I guess she didn't think she had the right to go crazy when I did the same thing."

To portray only closely knit families who respond in a supportive way would ignore the many other families who do not behave in that manner. Some families are so torn apart by constant turmoil that they have no energy left to deal with one more crisis. Sometimes the parents are divorced and they turn on each other, accusing each other of failing to bring up the girl or boy properly.

That, of course, is not the point. You know that you don't need your parents arguing over whose fault it is that you are pregnant. That just puts you in the middle of another battle, and it does nothing to solve the problem at hand. If your parents have always responded to a personal crisis by attacking each other or falling apart, maybe you should enlist the support of another adult in breaking the news to them—a counselor, a doctor, or a social worker.

How should you go about telling your parents in the first place? Part of the trouble may be the circumstances in which you choose to break the news. If you are coming in late from a date, and your father is standing there on the front porch fuming about your disregard for parental wishes, your shouting back that you're also three months pregnant will not put things in a better light. That would be like throwing gasoline on a fire.

Instead, choose a time when your parents seem relaxed. Perhaps after the dinner dishes are done, or after your dad has watched the evening news (everything pales in comparison to the evening news).

Rehearse what you want to say. You do not need to anticipate your parents' every reaction; you just need to know what you want to say first. Nothing is worse than getting their attention and then not knowing what to do with it. If you think your parents will react disapprovingly, it helps to know a little of what you plan to do in the near future so that you can tell them that, too. Knowing that you're not falling apart might encourage them to view the whole thing in a better light. Realize, too, that even if your parents go crazy when they first hear the news, chances are they will calm down and handle it better once they've gotten over the initial shock. Simpson said she had always marveled at how her own mother would fall apart when she dropped some unwelcome piece of news on her, but by the time Simpson told her father about it, her mom had recovered enough to keep him from coming unglued. Believe it or not, parents are human, too. They won't always take news of their teenager's pregnancy in a calm, welcoming manner, but they can come around, especially when they realize that they are needed.

In cases where the pregnancy is a result of incest, Simpson does not suggest treating the matter as described above. In such a potentially explosive situation, Simpson urges you to have with you an adult whom you trust to keep the situation from disintegrating into an ugly mess. The pregnancy may be a catalyst for your mother (or parents, depending on who is involved) to seek action against the perpetrator of the sexual abuse. Whatever the circumstances, you should not go through it alone.

At this point, you have determined that you are pregnant and you have told your parents. What happens next?

There is no guarantee that everyone's parents will come through for them. But if your parents do support you, you should have an easier time. Parents do not always respond admirably. Some girls who Simpson observed in counseling were actually kicked out of the house because they had become pregnant. Perhaps their behavior had continually taxed their parents. But whatever the reasons, they were out on their own, without shelter or resources, and seven months or so shy of having a baby.

Mia had that unfortunate experience. She became pregnant at fifteen, and her mother (her parents were divorced) told her to leave, to fend for herself. Mia moved in with some school friends, but they soon tired of her moodiness and her disregard for house rules. Other friends kept asking Mia to leave until she had finally exhausted all her contacts. Eventually, she wound up living with her former boyfriend's family, though she felt certain they were only helping her so they could find evidence that she was an unfit mother. Her mother never relented. Today, Mia has dropped out of school; she periodically finds stable living conditions so that the department of social services has no grounds to take her child away. It's a continuous battle, and she looks much older than sixteen now.

A colleague told Simpson about another case, but with a more positive ending. Jainey was also kicked out of her home by middle-class parents who disapproved of not only her boyfriend but also her decision to keep the baby. They said she could stay if she agreed to an abortion. When Jainey refused to have an abortion, they told her she had to pack her bags. Jainey turned to her friends, who took her in—at first. Later, she made her way to a women's resource center, where the staff members helped her find a place to live and money with which to finance prenatal care. Eventually, they helped her obtain child care. Jainey finished high school with their assistance. She also finished college five years later and had impressed her parents: they were in the audience at graduation, applauding like crazy.

Although getting cut off from family support makes it more difficult for the adolescent, it just means she has to turn elsewhere for emotional and financial support. The Department of Health and Human Services can help teenaged parents. Peer support groups can provide emotional support. The YWCA sometimes houses pregnant teenagers who are homeless. Family planning clinics understand that pregnant teenagers do not always have the support of their parents. The clinics know of resources where people can go to for shelter, prenatal care, and schooling. You need not give up your baby for adoption or have an abortion to be eligible for help.

On the negative side, families sometimes try to force teenagers into having an abortion. Remember: no one can force you to have an abortion. Instead of simply cutting ties to your parents under these circumstances, you first might listen to their reasons for suggesting such a course of action. Perhaps they can explain in a helpful way why they feel the way they do. Perhaps you, too, in a less heated exchange, can explain your own feelings.

If the two or three of you cannot come to any agreement, perhaps it is better to seek outside intervention to help you support yourself without succumbing to their wishes and then hating them for it.

ASK DR. JAN, PSYCHOLOGIST

First name: Tiffany

Question:
Who is affected during teen pregnancy other than the teen father and teen mother?

Answer:
On some level, everyone is affected. Most importantly the baby itself is affected not only by the health choices that its pregnant mother makes, but also by the teen parents' ability to provide adequate care after the child is born. The families of the mother and father are also affected. Additional emotional, financial, and child care support is often needed. This can be challenging for many families, causing increased tension and conflict. Teen pregnancy also affects the parents' friendships. Becoming a teen parent demands a tremendous amount of time as a result of increased responsibilities. Often, the parent (particularly the mother) is unable to hang out with friends as she once did and may lose contact with others as a result. The teen parents' educational future is also affected. More than two-thirds of all teenagers who have a baby don't graduate from high school. And ultimately we are all affected because billions of tax dollars are spent taking care of teenage mothers and their children, because they are more likely to be in the poverty bracket and require government assistance.

There are certainly exceptions to the rule: teen parents who are able to provide for themselves and their children with support from friends and family. Unfortunately for most teen parents, that's not the case.

Ask a Question

Do you have a question that you would like answered? E-mail your question to Dr. Jan at drjan@rosenpub.com. If your question is selected, it will appear on the Teen Health & Wellness Web site in "Dr. Jan's Corner."

If you have an urgent question on a health or wellness issue, we strongly encourage you to call a hotline to speak to a qualified professional or speak to a trusted adult, such as a parent, teacher, or guidance counselor. You can find hotlines listed in the For More Information section of this book, or at www.teenhealthandwellness.com/static/hotlines.

Some girls are too young to resist their parents' wishes, and it is certainly true that in some circumstances the parents do not want the best for their children. If things are done against your wishes, you are not likely to forgive or forget anytime soon. A nurse at a local hospital told Simpson of a case in which the parents of a teenager in labor decided that their daughter should give up her baby for adoption. The nurse had no argument with the plan; after all, the girl was only thirteen. However, the nurse had been instructed to take the newborn infant away before the girl could see it and change her mind. The nurse felt cruel taking the baby away from the girl, who acted as if she had no say in the matter.

Some families, although offering support and shelter for the single mother, send mixed messages at the same time. Gail, who was sixteen years old, told Simpson that her parents had been great and that they even fixed up a room for the coming infant. But her brothers missed no chance to shame her about her pregnancy. Her older brother said to her one night, "So that's what you've been doing with Jack in your spare time."

One woman had a daughter who had moved out to live with her boyfriend against her parents' wishes. Learning that Linda was pregnant, Sally drove to the next town to talk to her daughter. She offered to let Linda come back home to receive prenatal care and emotional support. Linda agreed, especially because her boyfriend had recently abandoned her. Although she may not have felt she was returning home under the best of circumstances, she was relieved not to have to worry about health care during her pregnancy or where she would live once the baby was born. Sally had not approved of what Linda did, but she decided it did no one any good to condemn the baby for the mother's mistakes.

Linda was angry that her mother had to rescue her and that her boyfriend had turned out to be such an irresponsible jerk. But because she was more mature than most teenagers, or perhaps because she had grown up in a loving household, she was able to accept the situation. When she had the baby, her mother was with her through labor and delivery.

When Linda was asked how that felt, she replied, "Well, it wasn't like I'd imagined it to be. I always thought my husband would be going through childbirth with me. But I was glad Mom was there because she made me feel that everything would be OK in the end. Sometimes now, though, I get a little angry at her—like maybe I think she's kept me from being independent. But I wasn't all that independent living in that apartment. Maybe by Mom's helping me now, I'll eventually be independent."

Then Linda smiled and added, "I hope my daughter behaves better as a teenager than I have."

Another girl had a different reaction. Diana never had a close relationship with her mother. In fact, they had a long-standing battle, with her mother accusing her of promiscuity and Diana accusing her mother of pushing her into it. When Diana found out that she was pregnant and her boyfriend refused to marry her, she assumed that her parents would take care of everything, even if they were not particularly happy about it. Though her mother suggested at first that she give the baby up for adoption, when Diana refused, she accepted her daughter's decision. However, she made it clear that she was finished with raising kids and was not about to incorporate Diana's baby into the family as if it were her own. She told Diana that it was in her best interest to live with a relative to have the baby so that the neighbors wouldn't talk, but Diana felt that her mother was rejecting her. Diana's parents provided well for her materially, but when it came to emotional support that had to come from Diana's aunt, with whom she lived until the baby was born.

Diana had mixed feelings about her family's support. She could not fault them in the matter of financial help (they had paid for all her maternity clothes, the baby's clothing and supplies, and her prenatal care and delivery), but she still felt they had cast her aside. She sensed that she had let them down, too, that she had done something wrong and set a bad example for her younger sister. She kept playing back her mother's words: "You're not going to ruin my life, too, Diana."

Some of you who have had no help at all, or parents with little financial resources to help you, may feel that Diana was still lucky, that at least she was not without financial assistance.

Here's another case where the teenager (a guy this time) lost the support of his mother because she could not condone what he was doing. Corey had never had a girlfriend until he met Trisha. After they had been dating a while and had become sexually involved, Trisha's mother found out and demanded that they marry. By then, Trisha was pregnant, though there was a question as to who was the father. Corey dropped out of school, intending to support his pregnant girlfriend. His mother, Margaret, a single parent of five, said, "I didn't approve of this marriage, and I wasn't going to participate in his mistake."

Corey married Trisha, but from day one there were problems. Corey was being battered, and he alternately went home to his mother to recoup from the abuse and then returned to his wife to endure another round.

1. How much family support do you have?
2. Has your own childhood been chaotic? Has it been scary or confusing because of financial instability or sexual, physical, or substance abuse?
3. How do you plan to make a more peaceful life for yourself right now?
4. How have you dealt with your past?

DISCLAIMING YOUR FAMILY

Finally, his mother refused to let him come back unless he agreed to divorce Trisha. Margaret said she wanted Corey to wake up and see what was happening to his life. She thought that if she withdrew her support until he got himself out of the situation, he would be more likely to come to his senses. She sadly told Simpson, "I guess he thinks I deserted him, but I had to do what I thought was right."

Corey told me that he did indeed feel deserted, not only by his mother but also by his siblings, who did not come to his aid either. Corey never actually tested his mother's resolve; he never appeared with suitcase in hand on her doorstep.

On a brighter note, Aimee married her boyfriend when she was a couple of months pregnant. Not only did her mother and father rally around the couple, but so did Bradley's parents. Aimee and Bradley moved in with his parents to save money, and Bradley continued

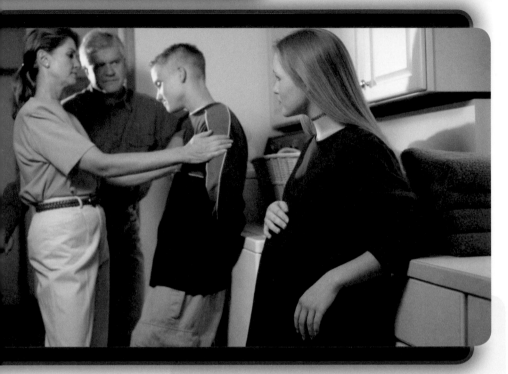

Siblings may have difficulty accepting your pregnancy. Give them time to adjust to the change, and try to involve them in your baby's life so that they will feel that they are part of the family.

to attend high school and work to help with expenses. Both sets of parents encouraged the couple to finish high school. By helping pay some bills and watching the baby after she was born, they made it possible for the teenagers to do just that. They have both graduated, have a lovely baby girl, and are buying a house. Aimee and Bradley beat the odds by establishing a solid marriage, although it was conceived in a hurry. They would probably tell you that it would not have been possible without their parents' support and encouragement.

YOUR RELATIONSHIP WITH YOUR SIBLINGS

Two main problems often occur between siblings when one of them becomes pregnant. First, siblings may resent you and the baby for getting all the attention. They may sabotage your efforts to get the baby to sleep or eat properly. They may refuse to help with babysitting or to keep the noise level down. Actually, they are probably feeling lost or left out. They need to be reminded that they, too, are an important part of the family.

There are ways to handle their behavior, including the following:

- Ignore it if it's not too bad. They may need time to get used to all the changes. You may want to offer to leave with the baby at times so that they can have some privacy at home.
- Involve them with the baby so that they will grow to love him or her, too.
- Speak to them when they seem to be purposely making things difficult for you. Seek solutions to the conflict that will help you live peacefully together.

Problems also occur when siblings try to take over the parenting of your child. They may even compete with you for the baby's love and attention. Again, they are trying to find a role for themselves within the family. Perhaps they genuinely want to help but are not sure how. If this happens, consider taking the following steps:

- Check to see that you are not delegating your responsibilities for the baby to them. If you encourage your siblings to take care of your baby all the time, you cannot complain when the baby prefers their company to yours.
- Talk frankly with them about their roles and how they can help you. If you think they are hurting your relationship with your baby, ask them to give you some time alone with your child.
- If you live with your family, consider moving to a place where you and your child can have more privacy and independence.

It is challenging to renegotiate roles when you still live at home with a baby. Be sensitive to the fact that everyone's lives are changing now. By talking together and working to solve problems with your parents and siblings, you can build a healthy, supportive family for your child.

CHAPTER 8

Simpson recounts that when she was first pregnant, she must have bought every book available that described the symptoms of pregnancy. She read them so frequently that she memorized whole passages. She was looking for some authority in those books to assure her that she was normal, that her feelings were not so very different from those of other pregnant women.

Simpson was not just comparing major symptoms or worrying about everyday things. She had a lot of vivid dreams. While her husband was preoccupied with how he would measure up as a father, Simpson was preoccupied with how she would hold up during labor—or even survive it. She wondered whether anyone else in the world felt as she did.

Fortunately for Simpson, the books concluded that someone did. Not all the books mentioned every single symptom and fear that she had, but among twenty-five books Simpson could usually find someone who had been in her shoes. It was reassuring to know that having a baby was not so new that someone else had not already experienced it all. That may sound funny to you. There she was, newly pregnant and already scared to death about labor. She thought she was the only person in the world who wondered if she could die.

One day a colleague's fourteen-year-old client announced that she was pregnant. Later the girl asked her therapist, "Does anyone die in childbirth anymore?"

Needless to say, other people do wonder about dying, and if it has ever flitted through your mind, don't worry. It does not mean that you're having a bad premonition or have jinxed your delivery. You are simply having a normal, frightened reaction. After all, you don't know your threshold of pain, and you don't know what your labor will be like. It is perfectly normal to be scared of unknown things.

You can do something about your fears; you need not live with them day in and day out. First, you should begin prenatal care as soon as you suspect you might be pregnant. Having a doctor monitor your pregnancy and give up drugs and alcohol, which can cause birth defects; these steps will ease your mind about your baby's development. As for your own well-being, become an expert on yourself: your strengths, your weaknesses, and your concerns. You can help your doctor by alerting him or her to your symptoms and fears. Share them with your doctor and the nurses who treat you. Make a list of questions to ask them about issues that bother you. If you don't ask, doctors may assume that you have no questions. Rare is the doctor who will take the time to pry questions out of a reluctant patient.

Sometimes you may not know what is bothering you, only that something is. It is still important to explain that to the doctor; most likely, he or she has had similar young patients and can help interpret what is upsetting you. Between visits, read as much on pregnancy as you can. Usually, the more you read, the more questions you will have. It is better to ask the questions now, when everyone is relaxed and unhurried, than when you're on the delivery table, saying, "Just a minute, I have a question. Just how much is this going to hurt anyway?" Before Simpson became pregnant, she had worked with doctors all her adult life. They were psychiatrists, not obstetricians, but she still knew that doctors were no less human than the rest of the staff. When you become pregnant, however, suddenly everything changes. Many women just naturally assume that the doctor knows best.

On one level, Simpson knew that doctors were mortals and had bad days. On a very different level, though, she expected them to be omniscient about her pregnancy. She was embarrassed to ask questions for two reasons: She might say something stupid and make them laugh at her, and she might waste their valuable time with small concerns.

If a doctor trivializes your concerns, you need to switch doctors. The doctor is there to serve you. You keep him or her in business. You actually make his or her job easier by asking questions, pointing out your concerns, and demonstrating that you are not a passive patient who will blindly accept everything he or she says.

When Simpson realized that the doctor was not taking her seriously, she took a good look at her own behavior. She discovered that when she took herself more seriously, questioning the things she did not understand,

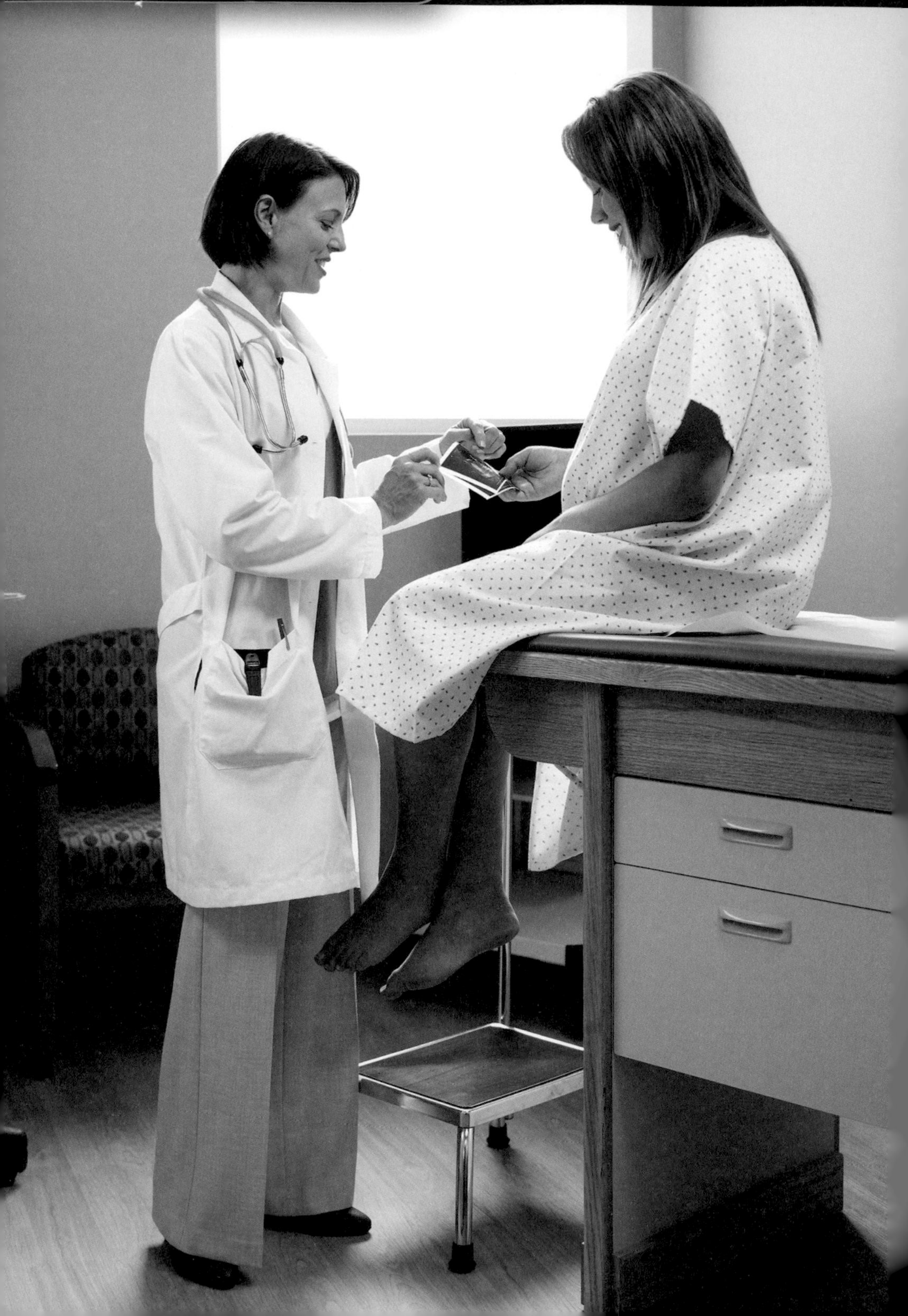

the doctor took her more seriously. Do not expect your doctor to be a god. He or she is a professional with whom you are working. The fact that you are younger than many pregnant women does not mean you have no right to be fully aware of your treatment.

Lamaze classes are another source of information and support. You attend these classes in your last trimester, when the information about childbirth will be of more interest and relevance. Taking these classes does not mean you have to have an unmedicated labor. Of the ten couples in Simpson's Lamaze class, only two women had babies naturally. The others were just as happy with their anesthesia and Cesarean sections.

The aspect Simpson liked best about the classes was the sense of having others go through this experience with her. Your friends can stand only so much talk about the baby or the pregnancy blues, but at these groups, Simpson and the other participants were gathered together for that specific purpose. Even now she looks back on those other couples as allies.

You may have heard pregnancy referred to as a roller-coaster ride. An objection to that comparison is that most people think roller coasters are fun to ride, and for some women pregnancy isn't fun at all. Be that as it may, Simpson gives a brief overview of some of the physical and emotional symptoms of pregnancy. Bear in

A teen discusses her pregnancy with her doctor. Don't hesitate to talk to your doctor about any concerns or questions you might have about carrying and delivering your baby.

mind that you may not have all these symptoms, particularly the emotional ones, because your attitude toward the pregnancy may be different. Do not interpret that to mean that no one else feels that particular way. It simply means that everyone feels differently while pregnant. Before you start worrying about your particular symptom, mention it to your doctor. Chances are you're as normal as they come.

Some women report feeling tired a lot when they're pregnant. Things people say make them want to cry, and their friends tell you they are more irritable than they ever were. Usually, these personality changes result from the higher levels of hormones coursing through their bodies. Less commonly, the moods are a result of their emotions about the pregnancy. If that is the case with you, it is helpful to talk over what is bothering you with a trusted friend, perhaps someone who has been in your situation. Some women "glow" during pregnancy. Their skin clears up (those hormones again), and they feel wonderful. Other women do not. Simpson was one for whom the whole experience precipitated depression. The only good thing about it was that she never had postpartum depression, perhaps because she was not attached to the pregnancy itself, but rather to the baby. How you tolerate your body's changes probably has a lot to do with how secure you are about your appearance before you become pregnant. Simpson had always been afraid of being overweight. (She was never so humiliated as when, in fifth grade, a salesclerk suggested to her mother that she look for dresses for her in the "chubby" department.) Periodically, her weight had gotten the better of her, but in her second marriage she had been very attentive to the matter. You can imagine her horror at seeing her belly take off on its own when she was pregnant. At first her waist got thicker, so that when she sat behind a desk at work she had to unsnap her pants so that she could breathe. She was too small for maternity clothes, but her regular clothes were straining at the seams. She considered making a sign to read, "I'm not fat. I'm pregnant."

Nobody told her that she was going to feel foolish wearing pants with a huge elastic front panel. The day she tried them on at home, her husband watched in fascination—no doubt wondering how long it would be before she filled out the roomy front panel. Simpson thought she saw him smiling. That was when she first considered getting dressed in the closet.

She remembered the first time she stood sideways at the mirror with no clothes on. She looked grotesque. She tried to suck in her stomach. Nothing happened. She pushed on it, and it was hard. Then she caught her husband staring at her from the hallway, and he had that awful smirk on his face. She tried to hide.

"Oh, come on," he said. "You look beautiful. I think your belly's beautiful."

"You're just saying that," Simpson said, but she did peer in the mirror to see if her sloping belly might look attractive.

It didn't. "Well, it's not fat," she assured him. "And it'll go away." "I know," he said. If anyone tells you that you look beautiful when your belly is growing beyond your control and you waddle when you walk, cherish that friendship. Your ego needs to hear stuff like that, even if you don't believe a word of it.

Simpson thinks the phrase that best typifies pregnancy is "loss of control." So many little things start to plague you once you're pregnant, things over which you have little or no control. To maintain your sanity, you need to decide early on that some of these things are just minor inconveniences. You will be running to the bathroom a lot in the beginning and toward the end of pregnancy. That is because your uterus is pressing against your bladder; whatever your bladder capacity has been in the past, it will be much less now. You may notice your breasts tingling at first, much as they do before your period starts. But this feeling will not go away after a few days. Your breasts will become fuller, and later your nipples will darken. Along with the darkening nipples, you might see a dark brown line down the center of your chest and abdomen, as if someone had drawn a mark to cut you in two. Books say that the line will fade but not always go away afterward.

Many people either feel nausea or actually vomit during the first trimester of pregnancy. Doctors attribute the queasy stomach to the increased hormones, which certainly will not make you feel any less queasy. Munching dry crackers or toast helps. If you can't find anything to munch on that you can keep down, tell your doctor. You should not go too long without nourishing your body. After all, your sustenance is the baby's, too.

That leads to another topic. Science has only recently become aware of just how dangerous chemicals such as drugs and alcohol (beer, wine, and liquor) can be to a developing fetus. You may not realize how crucial the first three months of pregnancy are to your baby's development. The fetus's brain, organs, and limbs develop in the first trimester. If you take something that alters the fetus's immediate environment, those parts of its body will not develop properly—and what does not develop on schedule will not develop later. Your baby does not get a second chance. Alcohol crosses the placenta; whatever you drink, the baby drinks. Your adult liver can filter the alcohol out of the bloodstream, but the baby's immature liver cannot. He or she literally swims in alcohol. Alcohol will affect your baby's brain development, and that is something that can never be undone.

Babies born to mothers who were heavy drinkers during pregnancy may have what is called fetal alcohol syndrome (FAS). They are smaller than other babies, have slower reflexes, and may have retarded motor development, impaired judgment, and other serious defects. There is no cure for this—only prevention. Even small amounts of alcohol regularly consumed by pregnant mothers may lead to babies born with fetal alcohol effect (FAE), which has similar symptoms, though to a lesser degree.

Don't take chances with your baby's life. Don't drink.

Smoking reduces the amount of oxygen reaching the fetus. Every time you inhale, the baby suffers. Since the fetus suddenly receives less oxygen, the baby may suffer respiratory problems at birth and be at greater risk to die from sudden infant death syndrome (SIDS). Researchers have been able to document the dangers of secondhand smoke. If you do not smoke but spend time in rooms or cars with people who do, your baby is still at risk. Breathing in a roomful of smoky air compromises your baby's development just as much as if you were the one smoking.

Babies born cocaine-addicted are often premature, no bigger than your hand, and suffer very real and painful symptoms of cocaine withdrawal. If you cannot stop using on your own, admit yourself to a drug treatment center. You are already heading for a hard time raising an infant at your age. Don't make things harder by having to raise a baby with severe health problems.

A friend of Simpson's suggested that she write about the physical complications of pregnancy, to encourage teens to take their doctor's advice seriously. She is a woman whose teeth were destroyed from lack of vitamins and proper nutrition during her frequent pregnancies. She now has heart trouble, brought on by lack of care in her teenage pregnancies.

"If I had been told these things could happen," Margaret said, "I'd have been more attentive."

"What would you have done if your doctor had told you these things?" Simpson asked. "Would you have believed him?"

"Well, no, I probably wouldn't have listened to him," she admitted. "But if literature had been available in the waiting room, I'd have read that."

From Simpson's observation, it is hard for professionals to impart any wisdom to teenagers, mostly because the young people are not always listening. Simpson knows that because she was once a teenager, and she didn't listen to adults either. But trust her on this one: doctors and nurses do know what they're talking about when they advise you about your health during pregnancy. It will not hurt you to follow a balanced diet and give up drugs, but you can be sure that it will hurt if you don't.

As you progress through pregnancy, you may find yourself increasingly fatigued. It's another one of those things that you will just have to accept. Some people feel a resurgence of well-being during the middle months, and of course, there's the proverbial burst of energy just before going into labor. If you're one of those who gets tired a lot, take frequent naps and rest as much as possible. There won't be much time for that afterward.

Depending on your stature, your waist will start to thicken sometime between three months and four and a half months, and eventually your belly will start to enlarge. Try as you may to hold it in, it won't budge an inch, and it will feel hard. Toward the end of your fourth month, maybe even into your fifth month, you may feel some funny fluttering in your abdomen. At first they will be only occasional, but as the baby grows larger and your awareness increases, you'll notice these movements regularly during the day and especially at night. Babies seem to be nocturnal creatures, but perhaps it's just that when you're lying still you notice the jostling more. In any event, don't count on getting a lot of sleep at night during the last stages of pregnancy.

Not everyone develops stretch marks. Simpson has had four pregnancies, spaced fairly close together, and had never had a stretch mark. Scientists say they have to do with skin elasticity and genetics. Stretch marks may look ugly during the pregnancy; sometimes purplish red lines running in all directions from the navel. But after the baby is born, they fade to pearly white and are relatively inconspicuous.

Some other problems will face you in pregnancy. Colostrum, or milk, may leak from your breasts after the nineteenth week in preparation for nursing your baby. You may experience hemorrhoids, varicose veins, frequent nosebleeds, headaches, nasal congestion, and swelling of your feet and ankles. Everything seems to get stopped up when you're pregnant. Your head hurts, your body swells all over, and it's difficult to have a bowel movement. Be wary of taking laxatives, especially before labor, no matter how many women tell you it will bring on contractions.

You can have weird dreams when you're pregnant. Women have told Simpson that they dreamed about themselves as mothers or about giving birth to a grotesque animal instead of a baby. Don't worry; it's just your mind's way of exploring your fears during pregnancy. Simpson's son was stillborn in her second pregnancy, and when she was pregnant with the following child, she worried that it, too, would die. One night she dreamed that she had the baby and it ran away from her. Only the baby was now a toddler who was climbing some stairs to get away. Simpson struggled to follow, but he kept getting farther ahead. Finally she got to the top of the stairs and saw a swimming pool toward which her baby was running. Just as certainly as she knew the baby would fall in, she knew she could not reach him in time to save him. Helplessly, she called to him to stop. Just then he toppled in, but right beside the pool appeared a woman who reached in and pulled her baby out. Simpson awoke with a tremendous feeling of relief. She knew that this time, even if her unborn baby experienced difficulties, someone would save him in time. And that is what happened.

At the end of your pregnancy, just when you are certain you can't endure another indignity, you may have a few more things to contend with, like a need to urinate even more frequently and sometimes failing to make it to the bathroom in time. Your navel will pop out, and you'll swear your belly will explode if it expands one more inch. People may accuse you of having swallowed a basketball. You may be embarrassed if you're wearing a tight-fitting (everything is tight-fitting at this point) sweater and these funny little movements jump across the width of your belly as if a mole were burrowing under your clothes. If you sit down on a couch, you may have to stay there a while until someone comes along to pull you up on your feet. You could get stuck in the bathtub, too. When you look down at your toes, they

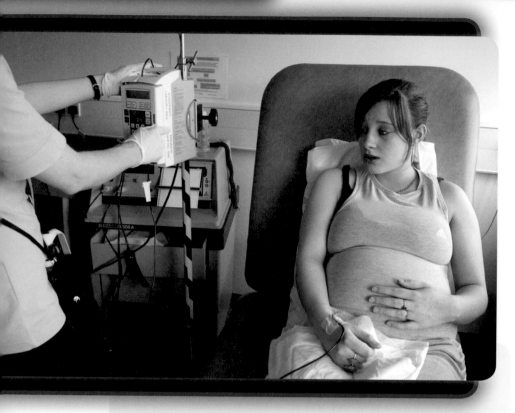

This teen mother-to-be became anemic (lacking red blood cells) during her pregnancy and is getting an iron transfusion. Anemia can make you feel very tired. Eating a healthy diet that includes plenty of iron-rich foods can help build iron in your blood. Ask your doctor about treatment options for your condition, though.

won't be there anymore. In fact, your feet will have disappeared, too. All you'll see is this immense, round belly overtaking your body.

When you are far along in your pregnancy, you may feel more dependent on others, such as your boyfriend, husband, or mother. That is a typical part of pregnancy. Women naturally feel vulnerable with a life growing inside them. Some women become nervous when their husbands leave to go to work. You may project your fear for the baby's safety onto your boyfriend or husband, so you worry about his getting hurt or killed and leaving you alone to contend with this pregnancy. It is a common reaction that usually passes after childbirth.

Pregnancy is not all bad. Some women truly feel a glow. They feel special and at peace, and it shows in everything they do. These women do not even seem to waddle in the last month of pregnancy. Do hormones upset them less, or is it their attitude? These are the women who caress their stomach and talk to the baby. They fantasize about the baby and themselves, and, in general, enjoy all the attention. They even enjoy the baby's every squirm, interpreting the punches and jabs as the miracle of creation.

Perhaps you are in the middle somewhere, marveling one day at this process of life and hating it the next. Nothing is black and white. Pregnancy is neither all fun and games nor a tedious undertaking. If you think the book dwells too much on the downside, that is only because you need no help coping with the good experiences. If you enjoy the whole process, good for you! If pregnancy depresses you, relax. It will be over soon, and you are not a "bad mother" for resenting the intrusion into your body. You do not necessarily hate the baby simply because you dislike the experience of pregnancy.

If you hang onto your sense of humor, you'll weather the whole thing with your sanity intact.

THE GUY'S VIEWPOINT

Even though the physical experience is out of your realm, that very fact may make the pregnancy all the more intolerable. You will watch your girlfriend or wife become moodier and perhaps more demanding. If you are not expecting this, you may take it personally. Make yourself aware of what happens to a woman during pregnancy. Realize, too, that these changes are caused in part by hormones and in part by the woman's positive or negative attitude about her experience. They may also reflect her being too tired to exert much control over her increasingly fluctuating moods. Pointing these facts out to her—even with good intent—usually makes matters worse. A woman already knows she is behaving unpredictably. It is no help to tell her it must be "one of those woman things."

Some guys are actually turned on by the sight of a pregnant woman. Not all guys are repulsed by the temporary change in shape. Some have told me they were afraid of hurting the woman or the baby if they continued to have sex. Unless the doctor gives a medical reason to abstain from sex (such as premature bleeding or pain), you should be able to enjoy sex all the way through the pregnancy. The woman's belly will begin to pose a problem after several months, but then you just have to explore other ways around it. You don't have to stop.

Some guys are very confused about their roles. They may ask themselves, "What should I be doing?"

1. Can you discuss all your fears with your doctor?
2. Do you know what to expect in labor and delivery?
3. Do you have a trusted person to go through childbirth with you?
4. Have you considered several options for medicinal relief if you're unwilling or unable to go through an unmedicated birth? Do you know what options are available?

EMBARKING ON PREGNANCY

That all depends on the woman. What does she want from you? Ask her.

Other guys treat their girlfriend or wife no differently. That is said to be partly because it's easier at first for a man to deny the pregnancy, which is not as apparent to him as it is to the woman, who can feel the changes inside her. About the time the man begins to notice the belly changing shape, he realizes, "She really is pregnant after all." Then he may start treating her like a fragile doll, just when she is enjoying the pregnancy and the freedom from those horrible first months of nausea.

As a couple, you can do several things to lessen the trauma of becoming parents. First of all, both of you must open up. Tell each other how you are feeling, what you are worried about, what you feel good about. Guys do not automatically know how it feels to be pregnant just because they've seen their sister or their mother go through it. All women are different; she must tell you what it's like for her. You cannot know what your wife or girlfriend thinks unless you ask her to share her feelings.

During Simpson's third pregnancy, she kept a journal of her feelings. She noted every little nuance; she wrote down every single thought she had. After a few weeks, she noticed that she was always writing about what the experience was like for her. Over all those pages there was no note of what her husband was feeling about this pregnancy. She remembered wondering, "Is he not talking to me, or am I just not listening?"

For your own information as well as to support your wife or girlfriend, you should try accompanying her to the doctor appointments. Some doctors are more attentive when a support person is with a pregnant teen, perhaps because the doctor feels monitored by a third party. Whatever the circumstances, take time out, guys, to go with her to the doctor. You'll learn a lot and be that much more at ease when you face the doctor in the delivery room.

Take Lamaze classes with your wife or girlfriend. These groups are a wonderful source of information and support. Sometimes men seem to benefit most because other guys are in the same circumstances. The classes can help prepare you for the surprises of labor, but you must not expect your wife or girlfriend to follow exactly any scenarios you've been told about.

Simpson remembered her husband phoning their Lamaze instructor while she was in the middle of labor. She heard him holler into the phone, "She's not doing the breathing right; it's not going according to plan."

Well, of course it wasn't; childbirth never follows anyone's plan. The classes merely give you a format to ask questions about pregnancy and delivery. You learn special relaxation techniques to prepare you for labor and help tune in to each other. Enjoy these classes and the people in them. They are there to help.

As a pregnant teen, if you don't have the support of your boyfriend or the interest of your husband, find someone else to go through the experience of childbirth with you: your mother, a trusted friend, or a sister. This is a time when you need all the support you can get. You can always use the positive energy of someone you love and trust.

CHAPTER 9

GETTING PRENATAL CARE

Some teens do not realize how important it is to see a doctor for regular checkups the entire time they're pregnant. You risk your baby's health (not to mention your own) if you fail to seek prenatal care early in your pregnancy. As reported in 2010 by the Guttmacher Institute, 7 percent of teen mothers do not receive prenatal care or they receive it very late in their pregnancies. The report also noted that babies born to teens are more likely to be newborns of low birth weight than infants born to women who are in their twenties or thirties.

Why would anyone not get prenatal care? For one thing, some teens probably don't consider it all that important. Some think they need only take vitamins. Other teens don't have the money to see a doctor. A private doctor is expensive, but family planning clinics will monitor a pregnancy for little or no charge. Social workers will also help teens file for Title IXI (Medicaid) benefits so that the government will pay for doctor expenses.

A baby is a fragile work of art. You, the mother, can do irreparable harm in the first three months of pregnancy when the fetus is developing its limbs and organs. You can also hurt yourself (sometimes fatally) if you leave some conditions (like high blood pressure or diabetes) untreated during a pregnancy.

HEALTH CARE VISITS

During the first visit, the doctor or nurse runs a pregnancy test on your blood or urine to confirm the pregnancy. The doctor then examines you internally, with one hand pressing on your abdomen, and the other hand inside the vaginal canal. She is checking to see if your uterus is enlarged. You are weighed (because they want a starting point) and possibly measured (to determine how your abdomen is expanding). A nurse takes some vials of your blood and sends them to the lab for testing. Your doctor needs to know several things.

First, she needs to know your blood type (and it's not enough to simply tell them what you think it is). She also needs to know your RH factor. Everyone's blood is typed either RH-positive or RII-negative. It is important to know if the mother is RH-negative. Complications arise when the mother's blood is negative and the baby's blood is positive. Incidentally, the reverse is not a problem. If a doctor knows that a woman is RH-negative, he or she will administer a shot after delivery to prevent antibodies from building up in future pregnancies that can cause a miscarriage.

Your doctor needs to find out if you are immune to rubella (German measles). Rubella can cause severe deformities in a developing fetus. Finally, she needs to discover whether you are HIV-positive or have other sexually transmitted diseases. Clearly, the blood tests are vital in safeguarding you, the baby, and the health care workers who assist in your delivery.

A pregnant sixteen-year-old is having an ultrasound reading to determine the size and position of her baby. Doctors can use ultrasound scans to diagnose certain structural abnormalities in the fetus, such as spina bifida, a defect in the spine.

Your doctor will also try to determine your due date, and that is not always as easy as it sounds. Many teenagers do not recall the date of their last period. Some are not yet having menstrual periods with any regularity, which makes it harder to determine just when they became pregnant. Usually, the doctor determines your due date by taking your last menstrual period (LMP) and adding nine months to that. However, in subsequent visits, she may order an ultrasound reading to determine fetal size and expected due date. It is not unusual to be off by a month.

Then your doctor (if he or she detects any health problems) prescribes appropriate medications, extra iron if you are anemic, and vitamins.

Your pregnancy is divided into three trimesters (tri = three, and three times three is nine months). The first trimester is the most important time (and the most dangerous time) to the developing fetus. This is when it develops its limbs and organs. If the mother drinks alcohol, smokes, or abuses drugs, the fetus may not develop properly. What does not develop at this time will not develop later. The damage is irreparable, meaning that it cannot be undone. For this reason, doctors will advise you to avoid all drugs (except those prescribed for you), avoid smoking (including hanging around in smoke-filled rooms, which is even more toxic to your lungs and the fetus's), and avoid alcohol. It's also recommended that you avoid crowds (especially where there are children who might expose you to rubella) if you have not had the MMR vaccine or a case of rubella yourself.

If you continue to smoke or drink, be honest with your doctor and nurse. It does no good to pretend otherwise.

During the middle trimester (months four through six), you are relatively free from discomfort and probably a lot less worried for the developing fetus. During your monthly doctor visits, health care staff members will be weighing you and measuring your belly to determine how well the baby is growing and if you are gaining too much or too little weight. Getting too big too fast suggests that you may be carrying twins.

Not getting any bigger may suggest that something is wrong with the baby or your diet. You need to eat nutritious meals (such as plenty of fruits and vegetables, whole grains, and dairy), even if you think you need to lose weight. Pregnancy is no time to start dieting.

By the time the last trimester rolls around (months seven through nine), most teens are receiving prenatal care. Some are just starting. This is when you might see some problems, like abnormal bleeding, high blood pressure, and dizziness. These are serious problems (unlike the discomforts mentioned in an earlier chapter) and require the attention of a professional. If you are doing fine, you will see your doctor every two weeks in the eighth month, and then every week in your last month. She may order more ultrasound pictures if there is a question about your progress and due date.

An ultrasound picture is painless, though it can tickle. The technician or doctor applies some jelly to your abdomen and then puts the monitor of the ultrasound machine into the jelly, moving it around your belly. The monitor emits sounds that call forth an image of the baby, projecting it onto the screen. Most people can barely tell what they are seeing unless the technician describes it. After looking at the baby (to determine its health), the technician can measure its head to determine approximate fetal age (which may revise your earlier due date). The whole experience does not hurt at all.

Labor and delivery are discussed more thoroughly in a later chapter. Briefly, however, during labor the uterus contracts as the cervix (the outlet of the uterus) expands to accommodate the baby's body. The pain you feel is from the cervix expanding to ten centimeters—almost four inches, roughly the width of four fingers. Once the cervix reaches ten centimeters, the baby can move into the birth canal, and you can help push him or her out. Some people experience pain when pushing, but most feel relieved once the cervix is completely dilated and the pain diminishes.

Now is the time to ask about pain alternatives for labor and delivery. If you wait until you are in the throes of labor, you are not going to have the presence of mind to focus on your options. Make sure, too, that you know what happens during labor. It will not necessarily lessen your pain to understand what is happening to your body, but at least you won't be taken by surprise.

- Painkillers (like Demerol [meperidine]) are supposed to mask the pain. Because all medications cross the placenta, you will not be able to take as much as you might like to take to obliterate the pain.
- Tranquilizers (like Valium [diazepam]) are supposed to help you relax. They do not disguise the pain. But if your pain derives from being uptight, a tranquilizer would be less harmful to the baby than a painkiller.
- Anesthetics (like the epidural block) are used to numb the body so you don't feel the pain. When an

epidural is administered correctly, you will be free of pain because it blocks sensations from the waist down. The epidural is a shot given in the area around your spine. It can be given once you have dilated to four to five centimeters. Most severe pain hits when you are between eight and ten centimeters. A spinal block can't be given until you're fully dilated, which is at ten centimeters. Although you will feel absolutely nothing from that point on, you have really already handled the worst. A pudendal block is a shot given in the perineum, the area between your rectum and vagina, to numb it for an episiotomy, a surgical enlargement of the vulva that sometimes is performed. You don't get that either until you're fully dilated.

If you are considering using these shots to blot out the pain, the epidural is your best choice simply because it can be given early in labor. But there are problems with the epidural of which you should be aware. It is a difficult shot to administer. Therefore, an anesthesiologist, who is specially trained to give the epidural, must be on duty at the hospital when you go into labor. It also hurts because you have to assume a fetal position (curled up away from the anesthesiologist) and lean into the needle. Only if the pain of the contractions exceeds the pain of the shot will you want to lean into this needle. Lastly, the epidural sometimes works only on one side of your body. When that happens, you feel every contraction in one half of your body. It is better than nothing but can still be unpleasant.

- What do you think are good reasons to have a baby? What do you think are bad reasons?
- How old do you think a person should be before becoming sexually active?
- How old do you think a person should be before becoming a parent?
- Is marriage important in raising a child?
- How many children do you want to have? How many can you afford?
- Do you know why you chose to become pregnant in the first place?
- Were there any family circumstances you were trying to escape? Have those circumstances changed?

BEFORE YOU GET PREGNANT AGAIN

When the epidural works, however, there's nothing better. You won't be aware of any pain, and you won't feel groggy from the medication.

Anesthesia is the other alternative, but it is not done unless you are having a Cesarean section, in which the baby is removed surgically through the abdomen. Regional anesthesia is administered using the spinal and epidural methods of injection, and the mother is awake during the C-section. Using regional anesthesia can take some time, so if the C-section is an emergency, general anesthesia would probably be preferred by the doctor. General anesthesia puts you to sleep for the surgery. You may think it would be nice to sleep through labor and delivery, but it's not done for routine deliveries. There are many factors involved in labor and delivery, and your doctor will consult with you about the best choice for the health of you and your baby.

THE GUY'S VIEWPOINT

The following points are beneficial for you to keep in mind when giving comfort and emotional help to your partner, who will soon give birth to your child:

Make sure you understand why prenatal care is so important. If you have read this far, you know. If you want to be supportive to your partner, find out what she's going through.

Go to the doctor appointments with her. Most doctors will let you watch them weigh and measure her. It's a good way to feel involved in what she is experiencing.

Plan to be available when she goes into labor. If you are working, ask your employer in advance if you can take some time off when she's ready to have the baby. Plan on taking sufficient time. She cannot have the baby in under two hours simply because that's all the time you can take off from work.

Attend childbirth classes with her so that you know what to expect. You need not be her husband to be her partner or labor coach. You don't even have to agree to be her labor coach. If you are not able to leave work to be with her during labor and delivery (or you're not sure you can handle the scene), you can still go to childbirth classes.

If you are going to be in the delivery room, make sure you know ahead of time what you might be facing.

It will not help your partner if you faint in the delivery room because you were not prepared.

Remember above all else, if you choose to support your partner during labor and delivery, you are her advocate. When she is in pain, she will not be able to think straight. It will be up to you to know what type of pain relief she wants and when to ask the doctors for it. To do that, you must know what the options are, and which are her choices. Make sure you talk together about all these issues.

CHAPTER 10

MAKING PREPARATIONS FOR THE BABY

This section looks at what happens once you become a parent. Of course, that means taking you from the last idealistic days of your pregnancy right up through delivery when reality starts to sink in. If you're an adolescent who seems to have idealistic and glamorous notions of young married life, as though it's full of only love and sex, you'll have a rude awakening about the harsh realities of parenting.

If you feel overwhelmed by the responsibilities of parenthood, don't despair. Many people have been first-time parents and felt stressed at some point. You can check out the Visiting Nurse Associations of America Web site (http://www.vnaa.org/vnaa/Searches/findvna.aspx) for referrals in your community. A visiting nurse can help show you the ropes and assess any other services you might need. It is not the nurse's intent to take the baby from you.

Simpson got the shock of her life when she had her first child. She thought babies were fragile, docile creatures that slept all the time. It never occurred to her that a baby could stay awake all night.

If you think she's painting an extreme picture of parenthood, you are in for a hard first year. It is better for you to know some of this stuff now while you still have the opportunity to take a nap when you need to. Or go to a movie. Or play music videos full blast. Take advantage of these freedoms now! Before taking a look at how hard it might be to raise that baby, you'll need to look at how much it's going to cost to deck him or her out. Have you considered what you will need, and have you checked out those classy baby stores? You will need to buy a ton of baby things, but they don't have to be the most expensive.

The hospital staff will not let you walk out the door with your baby until they see that you have an approved car seat. So that will be one of your first considerations. Find a car seat that is secure and easy to use. If it turns out to be hard to use, you'll find yourself using it less and less. Your baby's safety relies on this seat, but buckling the baby into it correctly is in your hands. Choose a car seat without twenty different sets of harnesses, and get used to buckling it each and every ride.

You will also need baby clothes—and a lot of them— unless you want to be a slave to the washing machine. Daily trips to do laundry can drain whatever energy you restore from a half night's sleep. In those first few days, it will seem as if you're always changing the baby. If your baby is a boy, it may surprise you how he can soak his T-shirt through without hitting his diaper. It doesn't really matter what brand of clothes you buy. You buy what you can afford, realizing of course that the baby will outgrow the clothes many times that first year. Depending on the season, you might even get away with just shirts and diapers. Let your mother or grandmother buy that expensive little sailor suit or dress. You need your money for more practical things, such as a crib.

There's no law that says you must have a brass crib or one of those fancy white-painted jobs. Remember, the baby cares less about being in a designer crib than being in a loving home. You and your friends will notice the setting; the baby won't. Try to look for a Consumer Product Safety Commission label that the crib conforms to safety standards. The most important thing is to make sure the crib bars are no more than 2 $3/8$ inches (6 cm) apart. A baby can squeeze through wider bars and choke.

Invest in a good mattress. You can pick up some items secondhand, but you're better off buying a new mattress. Mattresses break down easily, and you want your baby sleeping on a firm one. A mattress that is too small will leave a gap along the side or end of the crib, and a baby's head can get caught, causing suffocation. (According to the Consumer Product Safety Commission [http://www.cpsc.gov], if you can fit more than two fingers between the edge of the mattress and the crib side, the mattress is too small.) Don't bother with decorative pillows for the crib—decorative pillows can obstruct a baby's breathing passages and can collect dust. Babies don't sleep on pillows and will in fact suffocate in them if left to sleep on their stomach. (Always place your baby on his or her back to sleep, which is the safest position.) Buy a pillow only when your baby is old enough to pick one up and throw it on the floor.

As if a crib and mattress are not expensive enough, you have to buy bedding and at least a couple of extra sheets and mattress pads. Little as it is, a baby can soak through sheets and mattress pads in no time flat. You also need a pile of receiving blankets; again, a baby boy can soak a blanket without ever touching his diaper.

You need a high chair (although some people use a baby walker alternately as a feeding station) and perhaps a stroller. Find a place to store the baby's clothing, and you might want a swing to get him or her to sleep when all else fails.

Have you priced diapers? They are not cheap anymore, partly because they have become the new designer item. Some people must think that the more colorful and heavily padded diapers are, the more effective they are. Other people say that a diaper should not be too absorbent because the baby will stay longer in a soaked diaper before you notice. Wet diapers breed bacteria.

There's certainly nothing wrong in buying blue diapers for boys or pink diapers for girls, but it's not necessary, and it does get expensive. Ultimately, you should pick the diapers you can live with; after all, you'll probably be living with them for a long time.

A fabric baby carrier is inexpensive and a good way to carry your infant around. Babies like to be held close, and that is not always convenient. The carrier leaves you free to do other things while keeping the baby close to you.

If you are not breast-feeding (also called nursing), you'll need to stock up on baby bottles and nipples. You cannot stock up ahead of time on formula, even if you know what brand your sister says is the best. Babies are all different and have different needs. Your baby may need a soy formula, or may be allergic to a soy formula. Wait to see what your doctor suggests before trying to take advantage of drugstore sales.

Baby formula costs a lot of money, and this is one area where you cannot skimp. Women have made deadly errors by trying to water down formula to make it last longer. Using too much water dilutes the mixture, destroying some of its nutritive value. Your baby's health will suffer; some have starved to death on watered-down formula. Do not shortchange your baby here.

The same is true for medical care. You cannot skip appointments simply because you think the baby is doing fine. He or she needs certain inoculations, as well as weight checks to judge growth. If you cannot afford medical care, special "well-baby" clinics associated with state agencies provide health care at very low cost. Babies can weaken and sometimes contract deadly diseases later in life because parents have not been diligent with medical appointments. Healthy babies stay healthy by continuing to see doctors.

It's fun to buy baby toys because it's fun to relive childhood. Most of the toys, however, are more fun for the adults at this stage. In the beginning, a baby likes human faces, bright colors, and most of all, his mother's voice. It is immaterial whether your baby has Big Bird in bed with him. Even before he gets to the stage where he likes that stuffed animal, he will cherish the box it came in much more. So if you must skimp somewhere, do it on

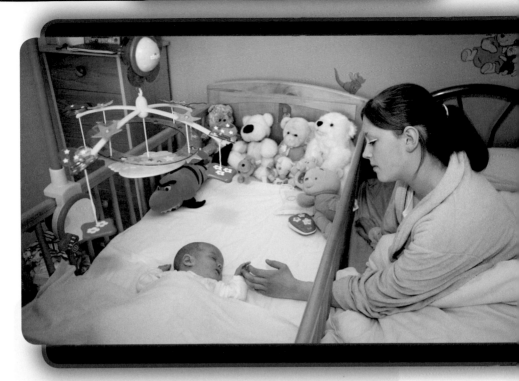

A teen mother watches over her two-month-old baby. If you share a room with your baby, make sure you have a spot that is the baby's space. A mobile suspended above the crib makes for a very colorful sculpture that is moved by air.

toys right now. That does not mean make the nursery a sterile environment. Buy mobiles or make them yourself (as long as they can't easily come apart and fall into the crib). Invest in rattles with different sounds and textures.

It's hard enough to buy all the things you need if you are both working and have saved up for the baby. If you are a teenager with little time to save and little family support, you may find yourself in over your head. There are alternatives, though. First of all, you must balance your wants and your needs. Looking at it that way, you can see that some of the "must-haves" for the baby are really things you just want to have. The baby can do fine without designer infant jeans. He will not do fine without a car seat and diapers and medical care. First things first.

It may help to make up a list of things under the headings Needs and Wants. Write down everything you can think of under each heading. Your Needs list may wind up longer than your budget, but don't worry about that yet. Put away the Wants list temporarily, and concentrate on the Needs list.

If you are a dependent on welfare assistance, a lot of the items are out of reach. Family services payments do not make for a cushy way of living, no matter what taxpayers like to believe.

Of your major needs, see which ones you can borrow from friends. Sometimes you can find good used furniture at garage sales or second-hand baby stores. Often these stores are run by mothers looking for a way to bring in added income without taking a regular job. They retrieve from their attics and their friends' attics retired baby items to sell at reduced prices. You can find some wonderful bargains without sacrificing your standards.

If you know ahead of time that you are going to be given a baby shower, let your friends know what you still need. If friends ask you point-blank what you want, don't hem and haw. Specify what you need. You can also start a baby registry.

Sometimes you can combine your needs and use one item for two purposes. A baby walker can also serve as a high chair, or a car seat can double as a baby carrier. A crib serves nicely as a bed and a changing table. But don't use the crib for storage of accumulating piles of laundry.

Just as a baby can suffocate in a pillow, he or she can suffocate under a pile of cloth diapers or T-shirts. With a little thought, you can eliminate some of your needs until you can afford separate items. A recent innovation is a padded insert that fits into a child car seat, making it a better fit. The padding, which costs less than $20, keeps you from having to buy two car seats: one for the infant, and a bigger one for the toddler he'll become.

Incidentally, people have become more careful about using baby walkers in the last couple of years. Many think they can be dangerous because babies have been known to topple over in them, severely injuring themselves. The danger apparently stems from parents using the walkers as babysitters. Unsuspecting parents stick the baby in his walker and then go about their chores or take a quick nap. Meanwhile, the baby kicks his little legs and shoots around the room, crashing into things he can't avoid and occasionally tipping the whole thing over—sometimes on top of him. If you decide to use a walker, stay around to monitor the baby's navigation. In addition, check to make sure that the walker conforms to the current safety standards.

Growing up means learning to live with your priorities and learning to do without. More than half the baby stuff you see on television is what advertisers want us to think we need. Babies never notice the labels. All they care about is being warm and loved, and that should be your priority.

THE BABY'S SPACE

Most teens will not have an entirely new room for the baby. When you have to share your room with a baby, establish a section that is his or her area. Work now to baby-proof the room, even though your baby won't be crawling around for months to come. It's easier to baby-proof now and not have to worry about it once your baby starts getting around on his or her own. Plug up those wall sockets, and keep cords short or out of the way. (You'd be surprised how fast a baby can pull a lamp down by its cord.) Finally, if you have a waterbed, never let the baby sleep on it. Babies have suffocated in waterbeds because they were unable to lift their heads up to breathe once they sank into the floating mattress.

Now that you have got most of the items you need, you are ready for the baby. However, you've got to go through labor and delivery first. Keep reading.

CHAPTER 11

CHILDBIRTH

This chapter looks at what happens to you emotionally as well as physically during labor and delivery. Some teenagers forget that this last part is the whole point of pregnancy. Small wonder: it's the hardest part.

Not all labors are alike. Just because your best friend took two days to have her first child doesn't mean you will do the same. Some teens have babies so swiftly and easily that they don't even make it to the delivery room, instead having the baby in the labor room or at home. If you are one of the lucky ones to have a short, relatively easy labor, bless your bone structure and everything else. But at this point, no one can know exactly how it's going to go. It's better to read through this chapter and be prepared for a more trying experience.

In general, you will have plenty of time to get to the hospital. A woman's first labor and delivery last on the average about twelve hours. Subsequent deliveries average eight hours. Remember, these are averages. Simpson's first delivery lasted twenty-six hours. Many people think that the breaking of the woman's water is the beginning of labor. This is not always the case. In all four of Simpson's pregnancies, the water never broke on its own until well into labor; usually, the doctor had to break it just to keep the contractions going.

For most women, the first sign that they are about to go into labor is when they lose what is called the mucus plug. All that amounts to is a slight bloody staining of the underwear. Sometimes it's a mucousy, bloody discharge, and it is not usually accompanied by contractions.

Another tip-off to approaching labor is that the baby stops moving around so much. If you have been bothered by the baby kicking you in the ribs and thrashing around at night, you may be puzzled by its rather abrupt stillness. It usually indicates that your uterus is gearing up to begin contractions.

Why does labor hurt so much? In short, the pain comes from the stretching open of the cervix to accommodate the baby's head and shoulders. The cervix has to open to ten centimeters, which is the width of about four fingers. There are three stages of labor and delivery: the first stage (the one that hurts) consists of the cervix stretching from 1 to 10 centimeters (0.39 to 4 inches); the second stage consists of pushing the baby out (exhausting, but not necessarily painful); and stage three consists of the expulsion of the placenta following delivery.

The first few hours of labor are deceiving. Once the cervix starts to dilate (stretch open), the contractions begin. Contractions are similar to waves of pain that wash over you much like waves at the beach. Sometimes there is a rhythm to them (which is why breathing exercises help); they come in waves every fifteen minutes or so. Sometimes, though, there is no rhythm at all. Some women say that contractions feel like really bad menstrual cramps. Between one and four centimeters, Simpson would have agreed. They were just like a bad case of cramps. But after that, she would have sworn she was in the grip of a gigantic vise. Some people feel the contractions in their lower back, not the abdomen. Back labor (as some call it) is very hard to handle, but having your lower back massaged relieves it. After four and five centimeters, it hurts a lot—which fortunately is exactly when the anesthesiologist can administer an epidural. Transition occurs between eight and ten centimeters; that is hard labor and the worst you will feel. The only good thing is that it's usually the shortest part of labor and it's all downhill from there. You will have trouble breathing through these contractions because they are closely spaced and very painful. This is when you will need your support person most because if he or she can keep you relaxed, you can manage the contractions much better. Resisting pain (which is a natural reaction) only makes it hurt more. It is uncertain why teenagers say they feel more pain during labor than older women; perhaps it is because their bodies are not fully developed.

Teenagers spoke not so much about the aches and pains of childbirth but about the nurses who helped them. If they grew accustomed to a certain nurse and her style, they often felt confused and abandoned when the shift changed and that nurse went off duty. Girls seemed to depend more on their nurse than on their mother or partner. If the nurse had a prickly personality, the whole experience became more stressful for the teenage mother, which made the contractions more intense.

You're supposed to remain relaxed during labor, so the pain will be less. It's hard to stay relaxed during a painful contraction. If the teenagers sensed that their nurse was more supportive than critical, they were more apt to follow breathing instructions and cooperate in the birth.

What about the girls' mothers? Nurses have said they were surprised at the number of mothers who came to the hospital with their daughters. Often these mothers reversed their whole relationship with their daughters, some of whom might have previously been kicked out of the household. Sometimes after delivery, these same mothers forgot the past and took their daughter and grandchild home to help with postpartum care.

Simpson says she can only speak for herself, but childbirth is not an experience she would have wanted to go through alone. It does not have to be your mother accompanying you into the delivery room; it can be your husband, your boyfriend, your sister, or your next-door neighbor. Hospital staffs are not judgmental about your support person; what they care about is that someone is there with you because a support person can make the experience a whole lot easier. He or she can calm and soothe you when you have had your fill of labor; he or she can encourage you when you're ready to quit; and he or she can indulge you when you need someone to scream at.

Terry went through labor with her whole family on hand. Her mother, aunt, and sister all stayed during labor and even through the delivery. At first it was interesting to have so many people around, but as the time dragged on and Terry became increasingly uncomfortable, her family members became more of a distraction. Terry resented their excitement about the birth; she felt as if she were going through hell while they were sitting around chatting. Terry told Simpson later that she had wished her mother had given her more attention during that time, but it's possible that no matter what her mother had done, there came a point in labor when the pain was so intense that it didn't matter what anyone else did. What any laboring woman really wants at that point is for the pain to end.

One word of advice: if you plan to have more than one person with you in the labor room, be sure the support people realize ahead of time that they are there for you, not to enjoy each other's company. If in the end they are distracting you rather than supporting you, feel free to ask them to leave. You need your energy for the birth, not to compete for your friends' attention.

Allison's mother stayed with her through labor and delivery, but right in the middle of the process, Allison's boyfriend showed up. Unfortunately, he did not know how irritable a woman can be in the last stages of labor. When he asked Allison if she would like him to stay, she replied through clenched teeth, "I don't care what you do."

Allison really didn't have anything against her boyfriend, who had not gone through Lamaze classes with her because of his work schedule. However, when she said she didn't care what he did, he figured she didn't want him around, so he kissed her good-bye and went to

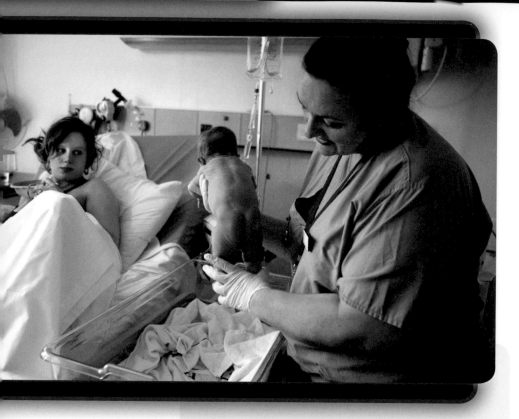

After the birth of a baby girl, a midwife looks over the newborn before handing her to her mother. It is great to have the support of friends or family during labor, but don't let the people with you become too much of a diversion from the delivery.

sit in the waiting room. Allison was then a little miffed that he had not understood what she was really saying: "I'm too wrapped up in pain to decide anything right now. You do what makes you most comfortable."

Labor can be a deceiving proposition. At first, when the doctor tells you this is the real thing, you may think, "Well, this isn't so bad." Simpson remembered her own first time, sitting on the couch at the birth center and thinking to herself, "Well, if this is as bad as it gets, it's a piece of cake!" A few hours later, the cramps moved around to her back and the pain got harder. "I must be fully dilated now," she said to the nurse, "because it's starting to get uncomfortable."

The nurse checked and said, "You're only six centimeters. You're not there yet."

Well, when all you're interested in hearing is that you're ten centimeters dilated, hearing that you're only six is grounds for throwing a tantrum. By the time Simpson hit eight centimeters, she had already told her husband that was enough for the day and would he please take her home. (Although she knew there was no way she could stand up at that point and walk out the door.) By the time she hit ten centimeters, she had not only sworn off having another kid, she had sworn off doing anything that would land her in this predicament again.

Once you are fully dilated, you're ready to begin pushing, which is the second stage of labor and delivery. You may want to begin pushing earlier, but resist because you'll tear if you start pushing before your cervix is wide enough to accommodate the baby. Sometimes pushing takes an hour or more. It's exhausting work, but oddly, it does not always hurt. If you have had an epidural or spinal block, you won't even feel like pushing; the nurses will coach you. The doctor will perform an episiotomy (making a small cut to widen the vaginal opening) if your vagina starts to tear (or to prevent tearing). Tearing feels like a burning sensation; the incision itself doesn't usually hurt (probably because the area is already fairly numb from the baby's head pushing against it).

Once the baby pops out (and that is often what it feels like), you still have to wait to deliver the placenta (again, a painless procedure). It hurts more to have the nurse press on your abdomen afterward to induce more cramping (which is necessary to help the uterus return to its prepregnant size).

SURGERY: A CESAREAN SECTION

Cesarean sections (usually referred to as C-sections) are not done because the mother wants to avoid a long labor. C-sections (which are major surgery) are done for four specific reasons, as follows:

1. The baby is either making no progress down the birth canal or is considered too large to fit through the mother's pelvis.
2. The baby is in a breech position (either buttocks or legs presenting first). The danger occurs when the first part of the baby is exposed to air. At that point, he'll take a breath. If the first exposed part is his buttocks, and his head is still inside, he'll gulp in amniotic fluid. That is why it's so important that a baby's head comes out first.
3. The baby is experiencing fetal distress (because of a weakened heart rate).
4. Meconium is present in the amniotic fluid. That means the baby has had a bowel movement in utero;

it is possible that he could ingest some of the meconium (fecal material) and contract a life-threatening infection.

If you need a C-section, you may have plenty of advance notice. In those cases, the doctor may want you to have an epidural block so that you can remain awake for the operation. (Don't worry, you won't have to see the cutting and stitching. In fact, neither will your support person, as he or she will be stationed up by your head.) In the event of an emergency, doctors use general anesthesia to knock you out for the operation. In that case, your support person will most likely be ushered out of the room until you're awake and recovering.

With a C-section, doctors make the necessary incisions (often trying to make their cuts below the bikini line so that no one need ever see your scar unless you show it to them yourself), and pull the baby out in the first few minutes. The rest of the time (usually an hour or so) is spent sewing you back up, layer by layer. Probably the worst part for many teens is the indignity of the pubic shave beforehand.

AFTER DELIVERY

Following a vaginal delivery, you get to hold your baby immediately. You may feel excited, proud, and relieved. It's surprising how much energy comes back once the contractions abate. You may want to count the baby's fingers and toes or just marvel at how small, yet perfectly

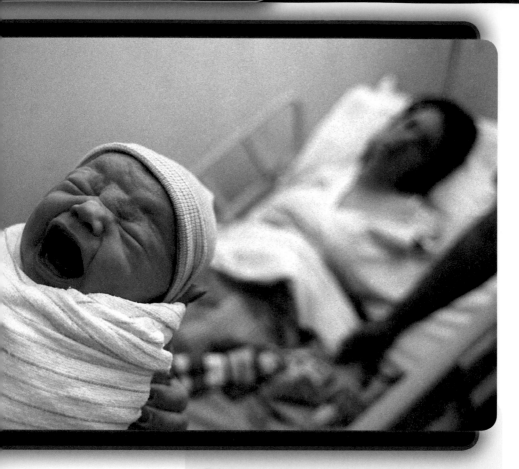

This teen mother was unable to hold her newborn son after delivery because she had a fever and cold. Immediately after a vaginal delivery, most mothers are able to hold their baby for the first time.

complete, he or she is. Don't be surprised, though, if you're just too tired to do much marveling or if you're a little sad. Sometimes people feel sad when others think they should be happy. Be prepared for anything; you have just gone through an exhausting, exhilarating experience. There's no set way to feel.

After a C-section, you probably won't be alert enough (depending on the anesthesia used) to do much with your baby. And you'll probably want to sleep more. Remember, you have had major surgery (whether you were put out or given an epidural). The incision will sting when you try to stand up the first few times. Then it will itch. You will be more fragile following a C-section, but with both types of delivery, you may be scared to use the bathroom that first time afterward. Don't worry. Your insides won't fall out, and though parts may sting, the pain won't compare to labor.

Some girls react to their newborn with fascination, confusion, adoration, and disgust. Yes, disgust. Bonnie told Simpson she watched the whole process of birth in the overhead mirrors, but once the baby was out and the doctor placed the bloody newborn on her belly, she recoiled in disgust.

"That was gross," she later told Simpson.

"But you watched the whole birth," Simpson said.

"That part was fascinating," Bonnie said. "But I didn't want a bloody baby on my belly."

Terry was confused when they handed her the baby.

"What am I supposed to do with her?" she wondered.

Karen had a different experience when she first saw her baby. "She was so purple, and the cord was wrapped around her," she told Simpson. "I was scared for the baby." When Karen had determined that the baby was fine, she said, "I felt like crying. Everything was over."

Just as you can have different kinds of labor experiences, you can also respond in different ways in the afterglow of the birth. Some girls feel a burst of pride—partly because they have created this new life, partly because they have survived the ordeal. There comes a period of "falling in love" when bonding occurs or is strengthened if it has occurred before birth.

A nurse working in the newborn nursery told Simpson about a time when she was sitting rocking a crying infant. Hillary, age fifteen, had just delivered a baby girl, and she came into the nursery. Hillary's baby was on the other side of the room sleeping, and Hillary watched the nurse who so ably quieted this infant.

"My baby is the quiet one over there," Hillary said.

The nurse had calmed the infant she was holding and was tucking it back into its bed. Hillary marveled at her ease with infants.

"Aren't they all so sweet?" she said. "I can't wait to have another one."

The nurse tried to tell Hillary, who was only half-listening, that some of those babies were "sweet" only because they were getting round-the-clock care by shifts of nurses.

Sometimes the lull of those first days in the hospital is really the calm before the storm. It can be alarming to bring home that adorable little infant from the nursery and discover that she does not sleep through the night. Or worse, to realize that no nurse is around to take over when you just can't stand another crying outburst.

The following are a few words about bonding. You may have heard that women feel this great maternal gush at childbirth—an overwhelming feeling of love for the child. That does happen with some people, but it does not always happen exactly that way. When Simpson's own daughter was born, she was so relieved that the pain had ended that she didn't notice the absence of any maternal flood of emotion.

When she and her husband took the baby home, she expected to feel something maternal, but she didn't. After a while, she interpreted her lack of bonding as a sign that she was a bad mother—mothers are supposed to be attached to their kids, and the fact that she didn't feel anything beyond a mild fondness was proof to her that she was unfit.

A few days later, when her daughter was hospitalized for jaundice, Simpson thought she would die without her. As the nurse took her out of Simpson's arms and she gazed at her daughter from behind the glass, she realized that she had indeed bonded with her and that was why she was missing her so painfully right then. Somehow outside of her awareness, she had bonded after all. It had not come through any great outpouring of emotion; it was just a slow process of falling in love.

Be careful when you compare yourself to other mothers. If you don't find yourself as maternal as you think you should be (and there's no definition for it), realize that this is a situation in which you have to learn as you go. Everyone has a different way of expressing herself, and most of the time, mothers mesh just fine with their babies. There are such things as personality clashes, and sometimes it is hard to bond with a baby who has a temperamental disposition or who is very different from

BREAST-FEEDING

According to the National Institute of Child Health & Human Development, an agency of the National Institutes of Health (NIH), the American Academy of Pediatrics recommends that women who don't have health issues should exclusively breast-feed their babies for at least the first six months of their baby's life. In addition, if they are able to, they should try to nurse for the first twelve months of the baby's life because of all the benefits to both the mom and the infant. A mother's breast milk provides the proper balance of nutrients to help a newborn grow into a healthy child. Research suggests that breast milk contains important fatty acids that help in the development of a baby's brain. Breast-feeding also benefits the mother because as the baby nurses, the mother's body releases a hormone that makes her uterus get smaller. There are also some emotional benefits from nursing, such as the intimacy of the act of suckling and the satisfaction of helping to nourish the child.

If a new mother has difficulty in nursing, the NIH recommends that she contact a health care provider who can help her find the assistance she needs with breast-feeding.

the mother. Let yourself love the baby in your own way. Have a trusted adult friend on hand to show you the ropes, if necessary.

Some teenagers are nervous about taking their baby home that first time, whereas others who have grown up caring for young children feel no special qualms at all. It will be challenging enough around your house in the coming few weeks. If you have someone to help you through the first awkward moments, you're one step ahead of the game.

THE GUY'S VIEWPOINT

Guys go through this whole process, too, whether they spend time in the labor and delivery rooms or wait it out in a different part of the hospital. Guys have mentioned feeling fascinated and overwhelmed at the experience of birth, especially that moment when a fuzzy little head first appears. Simpson said she has rarely had a woman tell her she cried at birth, but several guys have told her they did. It is a moment unlike anything else you'll ever experience. For most, it is an incredible bonding event, solidifying all the more your relationship with your baby's mother.

Not all guys react with fascination, though. Some get queasy seeing their wife or girlfriend's discomfort, and when it starts to get bloody, their knees may give way. If you are faint of heart, decide whether you will be more of a hindrance than a help. Simpson always encourages guys to be optimistic; they might come through when they least expect it. And if their legs turn to jelly, the nurses will get them out of the way.

For the guys in the waiting room, one can only guess that they're filled with equal amounts of curiosity and anxiety. Sometimes it's worse wondering what's going on than it is watching.

THE HOMECOMING

Childbirth is said to be the most difficult event a woman can go through. That is certainly debatable; Simpson thinks raising the child can be just as difficult.

You can do some things, however, to lessen the trauma. First of all, if you are confused about how to handle a newborn, how to bathe it or feed it, don't stew in your embarrassment. The nurses will be delighted to impart some of their wisdom to you. They can also arrange for a visiting health nurse to look in on you at home and see that you're doing OK. (A standard practice at one hospital is to arrange a visiting health nurse for all teenagers who give birth there. Karen was angry and embarrassed when the nurse showed up on her doorstep because she thought the hospital assumed she couldn't care for her baby. That was not the case.) Actually it is to your advantage that someone is interested enough to look you up rather than wait for you to make the call yourself. You can also call the Visiting Nurse Associations of America yourself (see http://www.vnaa.org for agencies in your area).

You can even call on your old Lamaze friends, who are first-time parents, too. Sometimes it is easier to struggle through motherhood learning things together. At other times, it's worse than the blind leading the blind.

If after your delivery you find yourself increasingly depressed, talk to your doctor. Sometimes it's a matter of trying to shoulder too much responsibility at once. Perhaps another adult or your husband could take over more of the care so that you have time for yourself. If your depression fails to respond to this sort of thing, however, you may have a hormonal disturbance that can lead to true postpartum depression. In this condition, you cannot will yourself out of the dumps. You need prompt medical attention and someone to take over much of the baby's care. Your energy will be needed for your own recovery.

Some people think they have to raise the baby in isolation, as if the task of mothering were so monumental that it could be done only by focusing all their energy on it, leaving nothing for a life beyond that.

This is no time to isolate yourself. Maintain your old friendships if you can. Find others who are in similar circumstances and share ideas.

If you did not have a nurturing family, it does not mean that you cannot learn about nurturing from someone else. Some girls who have a loving adult friend use her as a role model, salvaging years of their own emotional neglect. Remember, you cannot give something to your child that you have never had or known. Part of parenting is sharing early lessons of love. If you had few close moments with your own parents, seek out other people from whom you might be able to get that kind of feedback. You cannot undo your past, but you can enhance what you have now. Raising kids does not simply mean feeding and clothing them. It means nurturing them, too.

And last, but definitely not least, *relax*. Many women have been first-time mothers.

CHAPTER 12

MOTHERHOOD

This will be the chapter that makes you think, "My gosh, what have I gotten myself into?" If anything, this chapter may even make you wonder whose crazy idea it was to chance a pregnancy in the first place.

Some schools have a program in which teenagers become adoptive parents of dolls for a week. The students carry the dolls with them everywhere, and if they want a few moments without the doll, they have to arrange for a babysitter, just as if the doll were real. The idea is to give the teenager the feeling of caring for an infant on a twenty-four-hour basis. Usually, by the end of the program the teenagers are relieved to turn in their dolls and regain their freedom. It's a harmless lesson in the rigors of parenting. Maybe if every school adopted the program, fewer teenagers would risk pregnancy.

When Simpson was a teenager growing up in Maine, she thought having a baby was a grown-up thing to do, too. Not only grown-up, but sexy as well. Sexy because obviously it entailed doing something sexual to get one in the first place. There was one fleeting period of time when she would gladly have traded her last several years as a teenager to be grown-up and pregnant.

Today's teens are presented with mixed messages. The media may glamorize the lives of celebrities who have chosen to raise their children alone, but then report a concern about other messages, for example, in such movies as *Juno* (2007), in which the character, sixteen-year-old Juno MacGraff, has an unplanned pregnancy and chooses to give her baby up for adoption. Some of these outside influences can make it difficult for teens to make responsible decisions about the future.

Everyone has an idea about how his or her offspring will look and act. It is always in positive terms. People always think in glowing terms of the baby growing inside. Think back on what you were expecting. A spitting image of your boyfriend or husband? A little girl just like you to put in frilly dresses? Did you imagine that this little infant would sleep most of the day while you and your husband or boyfriend cut loose?

Here's the reality. . .

More often than not, the baby is cranky, maybe because he senses that you are nervous and unsure of yourself. In any event, he settles down only when your aunt, who has raised six of her own, comes to visit you. He falls asleep in her arms but manages to stay awake for eight-hour stretches when you are alone and dying for a nap. You are too nervous to breast-feed him, and he spits up the formula. You take him to the doctor, and the people in the waiting room say, "Oh, is that your little brother?"

When you get in to see the doctor, she sighs because she probably thinks you are young and incompetent, and all you want to do is get out of there as fast as you

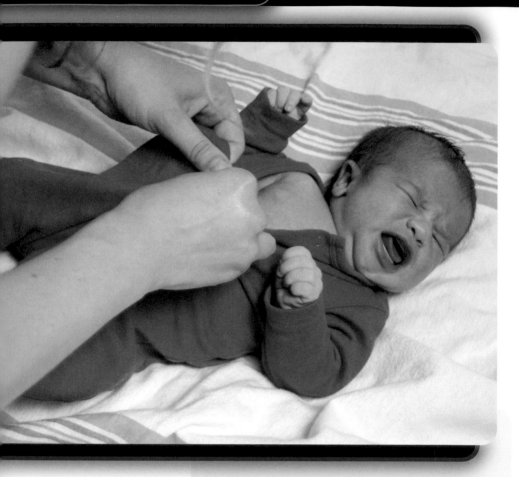

Caring for your newborn will have its challenges. Babies cry and can be cranky. Remember to have confidence in your abilities as a mother. But if you need assistance or guidance, don't be afraid to ask your doctor for advice.

can. You suspect she is noting in her chart that you are an unfit mother because you have not been able to clear up the baby's diaper rash yet, and the next thing you know she'll be sending a social worker to your door to investigate the situation.

Well, *relax*. Reality is not that bad, although teenagers can get carried away with their lack of confidence and their fear that someone is watching their every step (or misstep, as the case may be).

But reality includes sleepless nights for a while unless someone else gets up during the night to care for the hungry infant. Most newborns cannot eat enough at one time to stay satisfied for more than four hours. Hence, they wake you up for 4:00 AM feedings. You may be one of those people who can get up in the middle of the night, feed and change the baby (always do it in that order or you'll be changing him or her twice), and then fall right back to sleep. Most people, however, cannot do that. If the baby has a 2:00 AM feeding and then a 5:00 or 6:00 AM feeding, you will join the walking dead in no time at all.

Having your night's sleep interrupted can eventually make you psychotic. Before you get to that point, however, you will just be edgy and irritable, with the clouded judgment of someone fighting a hangover. Sleep deprivation can make you feel crazy. Simpson's first child refused to sleep for more than half an hour at a time. The only time her daughter was quiet was when someone carried her in a baby carrier, or she was riding in the car, or the vacuum cleaner was roaring underneath her crib. Simpson ended up driving around the countryside at all hours of the night because she couldn't stand to hear her fuss.

Sometimes when Simpson couldn't bear one more moment of wakefulness, she would turn on the vacuum cleaner, stash it by her daughter's crib, and lie down for a while. Sometimes she thought she would lose her mind during that period.

Having a cranky baby can cause chaos in other ways. Not only will she disrupt your sleep to the point where you don't know whether you've just gone to bed or are just waking up, but she will also undermine your self-confidence. You may start asking yourself, "Why am I such a lousy mother? Why can't I calm her down?" It's hard not to take that kind of behavior personally. It is important, however, that you be attentive to your newborn because an infant can become seriously ill so quickly. It does not require constant vigilance, but it does require attention. It might be useful to take some parenting classes at your local hospital or through the YWCA or a community center. Even if you are living at home and your parents are helping out with the baby, you need to know the basics of childcare and what to do in an emergency. Sometimes childcare books are especially helpful because you can turn to them over and over again.

If you happen to have a placid baby, or one who sleeps through the night from the moment you bring her home, you're more than lucky!

There is nothing glamorous about changing messy diapers. Pretty soon your whole world revolves around whether Junior had a bowel movement today or not, and it's no wonder friends may forget to include you in gatherings. They assume either that you wouldn't join them in the first place, or worse, that you'd bring the "kid" with you.

1. Do you have a concerned adult you can turn to if you become overwhelmed with childcare responsibilities?
2. Will you have any opportunity to get out by yourself?
3. How will you afford all the things your baby needs?
4. What will you do if your baby won't stop crying? Is choking? Isn't breathing?
5. Have you had any previous experience with infants? Have you taken any safety courses? Baby classes?
6. How do you plan to prevent future pregnancies?
7. How much do you know about STDs and HIV/AIDS? How do you intend to avoid contracting them?

BECOMING A MOTHER OR FATHER

If you have any time left for your husband or boyfriend, it may not be quality time. The baby typically gets all the quality time, and what is left belongs to you and your partner. Usually, before your husband gets that time, you've fallen asleep. Sometimes mothers are not very sexy creatures; they are so wrapped up in being mothers that they cannot always shift gears and return to being wives or lovers.

There's not much time for you and your husband, and sometimes it is too much of a strain to spend it nurturing your boyfriend or husband as well as the baby. Some men are outright jealous of the infant. The last thing a woman wants is another person to take care of.

GIVING YOUR BOYFRIEND ATTENTION

Making time for you and your boyfriend takes some planning and effort when you are a new mother. Taking the following steps may help you focus on your relationship:

Set aside time to spend alone with your boyfriend. Don't be afraid to leave your baby with a sitter if you can afford one.

Talk about your own lives, rather than always talking about the baby.

If you don't have time to plan something romantic, do chores together and talk. Go grocery shopping together. At least you can be together.

Turn off the phone and let the answering machine or voicemail take over.

For guys, the experience of fatherhood seems to be a shock. Their ability to throw themselves into the experience is related to the degree of commitment they feel to their new family and their own level of maturity. For some, a pile of smelly diapers is simply too overwhelming. Babies are not always cute. Single guys who are visiting fathers may be disenchanted with their girlfriend's preoccupation with the baby. It is hard to admit to competing with a baby for your girlfriend's attention; it may be easier to fade away from the relationship for now. That is not to shortchange you guys who are devoted fathers—some of you help out with the baby even after a full day of work or school. Usually, these guys are secure in their girlfriend's/wife's love and not insistent.

Nevertheless, Simpson believes that most guys are surprised to find that fatherhood is more tedious than they were led to believe. After all that attention lavished on the pregnant teenager, it's hard to play second fiddle to a baby, particularly a demanding, ungrateful one. Some days when people came to visit, bearing gifts for the baby, Simpson wanted to say, "What did you bring *me*?"

Reality is that now you're the mother and not destined to be the center of attention anymore. Even if you are blessed with a docile, happy baby, unless you have someone to help you watch the little cherub, you're going to be taking him or her with you everywhere, just as those students carried their dolls to every class and every school activity. Many people love babies, but they are not usually the ones who have to take them home at night. If you find yourself getting weighed down by all this one-on-one with your baby, find someone to babysit for a while before you start thinking of him or her as your "keeper." You can't leave your baby unattended just because he's asleep. That's neglect. If you want to go somewhere, you either cart him along or call a sitter.

The sad realities are many for married teenagers. You start wondering, "Where did the glamour go? Why

This teen mom is feeling the frustrations and demands of caring for a child. If you think you are on the verge of collapse or have reached a snapping point, contact your public health nurse or talk to a helpline such as that at Parents Anonymous to ask for counseling.

am I always so tired? Why don't we have time for each other anymore? Why does it cost this much to feed a kid?"

But there are also questions for single parents: "How do I start a new relationship when I have to take the baby everywhere? Where will I find time for another person in my life? How can I attract someone when I'm so tired all the time?"

If you are overtired and overburdened with childcare, as many of you without family support will naturally be, you are risking the possibility of abusing the baby—especially if you grew up abused yourself. You need adequate, restful sleep to think straight and react calmly. If you do not get sleep,

you are setting yourself and the baby up for explosive consequences. Seizing the baby in a sudden burst of anger, shaking him or her to stop the crying, can permanently damage the baby's spinal column and neck. It can cause internal bleeding and can even kill the baby. Just one unchecked moment of anger or throwing the baby down on the mattress can shake up his insides, causing internal bleeding or death. The baby's brain nestles inside the head. It has room to grow, but when a baby is shaken, his brain is thrown against the inside of his skull. This causes blood vessels to break. It can also create tiny tears in the brain that can ultimately affect his ability to think, talk, breathe, and perform other important functions. Because the brain is so delicate, it does not require a great amount of force to injure it permanently.

One well-publicized case involving a shaken baby centered upon the death of Matthew Eappen, an eight-month-old infant from Massachusetts. His parents accused their au pair (a live-in babysitter), Louise Woodward, of shaking him to death. A jury convicted her, but the judge subsequently reduced her sentence to manslaughter (unintentionally causing another person's death). Woodward denies shaking the baby hard enough to have caused his death, but doctors concurred that the baby died from injuries sustained from being shaken.

If you fear you are reaching the breaking point, call your public health nurse—if you have one—or Parents Anonymous, an abuse hotline (see For More

Information). Seek supportive counseling to learn better ways to handle your anger. If your baby's crying is pushing the buttons on your self-control, lay the baby in his crib and go outside for a moment (but not, of course, down the street or over to a neighbor's), or take a hot shower to calm your nerves. You need a break or a friend—or both.

Some of you may not think you would ever hurt your baby, but you still might worry that a social worker would investigate your home and accuse you of child abuse. It is frightening to think that others (like the social or family services department) have the power to take your child away if they believe you're abusing him or her. Usually, they have good indications of abuse, but Simpson has spoken with teenagers who swore they were not hurting their child, although it was clear that something was happening to the baby. One mother accused the day care center; the day care center accused the mother. Some girls are afraid that their boyfriend or boyfriend's parents will find fault with their handling of the baby in order to gain custody. It's hard enough to deal with normal, everyday anxiety about bringing up a baby. It's worse when you are constantly afraid that your youth will be grounds for losing your baby. That will not happen as long as you are responsible in meeting the baby's needs and are nonabusive (which also means not neglectful).

The way a teenager responds to her baby depends on several things: her level of maturity, for one thing, because caring for a baby means putting the baby's needs before your own. It also depends on how much support she has. The girl who has her mother or an involved husband with whom to share these new responsibilities will be fresher and more rested. And of course, it depends on the baby's disposition. Some babies are simply harder to deal with than others. It has nothing to do with you personally. It's just genetics.

A NOTE ABOUT YOUR PARENTS

For those of you who choose to live at home and utilize your parents' support (whether it is financial, emotional, or otherwise), be prepared for some trade-offs. Early on you must decide how much of a role they will play in your baby's care, and the three of you must agree on it. Are they going to act like grandparents or another set of parents?

If you abdicate your role as parent, you must not complain when they take over the role themselves. It is not fair to expect your parents to foot the bills and be the babysitters while you are off with your friends and then squawk because they have assumed a larger share in the childrearing than you wanted to give them. If you accept their help, you must allow them some say in your affairs. Getting along with your parents after you become a parent yourself is one of the most difficult tasks you will face. Sit down ahead of time, talk about ground rules, but realize that you cannot have it both ways. If you are going to be a parent, do not expect your mother or father to do more than a grandparent's share of the work.

On the other hand, if you find yourself in a constant battle with your parents over the baby's care, you may choose to live with someone else or on your own if you can afford it. It is undoubtedly more difficult managing alone, but intrusive parents who undermine your authority with your child may be equally destructive. If you spend more time fighting with them than raising the baby, it is time to reassess your need for their help.

CHAPTER 13

THE LOSS OF YOUR BABY

In 2005, the United States ranked thirtieth in the world in infant mortality (death), according to the Centers for Disease Control and Prevention. This chapter will probably be the hardest one for you to read because it deals with something going wrong in your pregnancy. In a report posted on Livestrong.com in September 2010, the infant mortality rate in 2005 for babies born to mothers under the age of twenty was 10.28 deaths per 1,000 live births, compared to the average of 6.86 deaths per 1,000 live births for all births. Many people shake their heads at the staggering number of teenagers giving birth each year—more than one million, according to some estimates. These same people seem unconcerned by the effects of the untold losses: In the United States, each year there are 600,000 women who lose their babies through miscarriage, there are about 200,420 abortions among fifteen- to nineteen-year-olds, and some 28,000 babies will die before reaching their first birthday. The deaths often occur because of the mother's inadequate prenatal care.

This chapter strives to help you recognize these losses, let you look at your pain, if you have suffered one of these losses, and then let it go. If it helps you to know, Carolyn Simpson lost a child, too. You may be relieved to know that she has survived the pain. If you have lost a baby, you will be forever different. For those of you who are reading this chapter because a friend has lost a baby, the greatest favor you can do for your friend is to let her grieve. And listen. And listen. And listen some more.

First, it will help to clarify some terms. Miscarriage is the expelling of the fetus before it is able to survive (from a day-old pregnancy ending in blood and tissue to a five-month pregnancy ending in a more recognizable fetus). A stillbirth occurs when an infant dies before birth, and a neonatal death occurs when an infant dies in the hours or days just following birth.

When a teenager loses a baby, most of society is relieved to be rid of the problem. Some assume that the teenager herself is too inexperienced in life to realize what she has lost, that because her circumstances would have been so negatively altered by the birth of the child, she is probably relieved to be rid of it. The main thing wrong with this line of thinking is that even if the girl were relieved, there would still be immeasurable guilt in feeling relieved.

A loss is a loss, whether it happens to a thirteen-year-old girl or a thirty-year-old woman. Neither age nor marital status insulates a person from pain. The older, more mature woman may merely be better at articulating that loss.

When Simpson was a junior in high school, a girl her age that she had grown up with got pregnant, married, and left school—in that order. It happened occasionally, so it really wasn't such a big deal.

Months later, Simpson and her friends heard that the baby had died at birth. For them, the shock lay in the unthinkable having happened. And then they thought, "Too bad Susan married so fast. Now she has no reason to stay married."

It never occurred to most of them that someone, a baby, had just died and that the parents—even if they were only seventeen years old—were just as shaken as older ones would have been.

Simpson thought of this girl years later when her own son died at birth. She realized with belated awareness how much pain her friend must have felt. It didn't matter that she was young enough to have more kids in the future. That child was gone. The loss, emptiness, and rage must have been there.

The reactions to a loss are as varied as the reasons for a person's getting pregnant in the first place. To some extent, your reaction reflects how important the pregnancy was to you or how real it had become. Simpson explains her own case.

Her son was stillborn when she was thirty-eight weeks pregnant. ("At term" is considered anywhere from thirty-eight to forty-two weeks.) Simpson had a normal pregnancy; she was healthy, had never smoked, and did not use drugs or alcohol. In fact, she had not heard of anyone in her circumstance losing a baby this way. The baby was delivered at 4:00 AM, and in a state of oversedation, she slept the rest of the morning. When she awoke, she couldn't remember at first where she was or why she was there. And then it hit her as though she had been punched in the stomach. Her son was dead. She saw tubes sticking out of her and liquids running into her, and she tried to focus on the physical pain to block out the ice-cold panic creeping through her. She thought of the words in a song: "Nobody knows it's the end of the world," since the sun was shining and birds were flitting by her window as if nothing extraordinary had happened that day.

After a while, the numbness started to wear off, and she went a little crazy from the anger festering inside. There was so much free-floating anger that she hardly knew where to begin. She hated all the people who told her not to worry, that she could always conceive again, as well as all the people who said, "It must have been God's will," as if anyone would have willed for a baby to die inside its mother. She even hated all the other pregnant women in the world who were going about their pregnancies.

Simpson didn't move through the stages of grief in any consistent manner. Some days she was so angry, she could barely see straight, thinking things like, "Why me? What have I done to deserve this?" Other days all she wanted to do was curl up in bed and sleep for one hundred years, and not wake up until the pain was gone.

"If I could just not remember," she told herself, but there were reminders everywhere: other infants, all the baby things she had accumulated, and the date staring at her from the wall calendar. Sometimes she thought the whole thing was a bad dream, and that if she could only wake up she'd see that her son had not died after all.

She felt guilty, too. Doctors never found out why her son had died. "It was just one of those things," they said.

So there she was, with all that anger and no one to blame. Part of her believed it must have been her fault. After all, she was the mother; she should have known something was wrong. Had she done something wrong? The night before their son died, her husband and she had argued about her overspending on baby clothes. Had their angry feelings somehow hurt the baby? Why hadn't she known? Surely that was her fault.

Coupled with the feelings of anger, shock, and guilt was the intense desire to conceive again. Not just to see if she could have another child, but also to rectify her failure. Maybe this time she would do it right.

The loss of her son was the most wrenching, horrible thing that ever happened to her, and yet society treated her with respect and caring. That was because she was happily married and stable enough to provide for a child. That support caused her to wonder about the unwed pregnant teenager, for whom an unplanned pregnancy was often seen as a negative thing. How would an unwed teenager get any recognition of her pain so that she would not feel compelled to rush right out and become pregnant again?

More often than not, society does not believe that you—the teenager—grieve over a miscarriage or stillborn child, nor does it typically believe that anything significant has been lost. After all, it is not as if you had come to know the child.

What society fails to realize is that you may already have bonded with the unborn child, with the fantasy of being its mother, and now not only is the child gone but also the promise of motherhood.

Of course, there are different levels of awareness and different ways that people respond to loss. The twelve-year-old who does not realize she's pregnant until an early miscarriage brings the fact to light will probably feel less grief than the seventeen-year-old girl who has wanted the pregnancy and loses the child after six or seven months.

For those of you who claim to feel nothing at all over your loss, Simpson suggests that you dig a little deeper into your feelings. Numbness and denial serve a purpose—essentially, to spare you the pain of awareness. Unfortunately, ignoring the pain or insulating yourself from it will not make the it go away. Neither will drugs or alcohol. You are never entirely free from the pain of loss, even if you choose not to look at it.

Simpson once worked with a woman in one of her therapy groups who told the participants one evening that it was her dead son's birthday. This woman was in her late sixties, but not a year had gone by that she hadn't remembered her dead son's birthday. He had been stillborn forty-eight years before.

Another woman, hospitalized and dying of cancer, told a nurse that she was not afraid to die because "now I will see my babies again." This woman had ten living children, numerous grandchildren, and even a few great-grandchildren. Still she remembered the dates of her two miscarriages (at least sixty years earlier) and her son's stillbirth. "I never stopped grieving for those babies," she said, although her life appeared rich with love and fulfillment.

For those of you who have suffered a miscarriage, stillbirth, or neonatal death, no one is condemning you to months of agony. What is hoped is that it's clear to you that losing someone hurts, and that it is OK to feel pain and anger, even if having that child might have seemed the most tragic mistake of your young life. Grieving will not kill you, and it will not torment you forever if you deal with it.

Speaking of guilt, what about the stillbirths and neonatal deaths caused by the mother's lack of prenatal care or her abuse of drugs and alcohol?

If this happens, you will have to confront the part you played, through ignorance or negligence, in the death, and then sadness and pain over the loss. Hopefully, you can learn from this tragedy and ultimately forgive yourself.

A special kind of loss comes with abortion because you have purposely chosen to terminate the pregnancy. Because of your decision, you have to separate the guilt before you can reach the pain. Many people opting for abortion deny that it was a big deal. Some admit that they regret it, but they are also quick to say that they had no other choice. It had to be done, as if its urgency negates the pain of loss.

The point is not that you should not have had the abortion (that is a decision only you can make); it is that

If you have lost your baby through miscarriage, stillbirth, or neonatal death, don't feel that you can't grieve for your loss. Friends and family members can help console you during your tragic loss—don't be afraid to deal with your sadness.

no matter what else, the unborn child was part of you, and now it is gone.

Over the years, Simpson has known many women who have had abortions. They were from every social class, though abortion tends to be more of a middle- and upper-class solution to an unplanned pregnancy. The one thing that all these women (including teenagers) had in common was their regret. That is not to say that all of them would have gone on to bear the child; most would still have had the abortion. However, their choice haunted them over the years, and they often wondered what the child might have looked like. Even though they had precipitated the loss, they still grieved over it.

One of the problems with abortions is that they have often been done in secret. You can't share your feelings with others when you have not revealed the event that caused them. Just when you need emotional support most, you may have closed yourself off by pretending the event never happened.

Faith was an attractive teenager when she became pregnant. Having been brought up in the Bible Belt of Oklahoma, she felt guilty and trapped by her dilemma. Having a baby as an unwed mother was almost as frowned upon as aborting it; the first was seen as rejecting the morals of the community; the second was violating the sanctity of life. Nonetheless, Faith chose to have an abortion in secrecy. She moved away from home to attend college but evidently never found the peace of mind she was seeking. She grew obese and used that as a way to avoid intimacy and the possibility of becoming pregnant again. Simpson last saw Faith several years ago. She had become very religious, and she rarely discussed what she had done. When she did, it was to focus on her guilt, not her grief.

A therapist once asked Simpson, when she was full of anger and self-pity, "If you took away the guilt and anger, what would you have left?"

For a moment Simpson was silent. What were the guilt and anger keeping her from feeling? And then it hit her, as if a truck had plowed right into her. Emptiness. Loss. It was much easier to be mad than to ache.

Anger is pervasive. You may be mad at yourself for not producing a healthy child, at your boyfriend or husband for making you pregnant, and at that same guy for not sharing your loss. (Sometimes Simpson felt that their stillborn son was her loss alone; after all, her husband had not shared the physical trauma of delivering a dead baby. He had not felt the life inside him during those thirty-eight weeks.)

Sometimes you may feel angry because no one seems to care that you hurt or that the baby died in the first place. And invariably you feel angry at everyone who has gone on to deliver healthy babies. Simpson never saw so many pregnant women or infants in her life as she did after she and her husband lost their son. She resented them all, even the infants, because they were not her son.

Several colleagues at Simpson's office were also pregnant when her son died. She felt she was being additionally singled out for punishment, having to face them each day. She even tried to avoid some of the women—and especially their babies, who only reminded her of her loss.

It was harder for Simpson to avoid her best friend, who once accused Simpson of spoiling the joy of her pregnancy. Ultimately Simpson had to confront and accept her loss so that she could keep her friendship. But for a long time, she was afraid to hold her friend's baby, afraid of her fears and desire, ashamed that she was being disloyal to her dead son. It took a lot of guts, not only for Simpson to hang onto this friendship, but also for Janet not to recoil from her experience.

You may have girlfriends who have carried pregnancies to term, and only you can decide whether you should struggle to maintain the friendships or put them temporarily on hold.

Believe it or not, even with all her ignoble feelings, Simpson was not crazy. And you are not crazy just because you have them, too. You may feel like snatching someone else's baby. As long as the vengeful fantasy remains a fantasy, you need not condemn yourself for it. You just don't act on it.

Anger is one thing; grief and longing are far harder to endure. After her son died, Simpson experienced waves of longing to hold him. There she was, over thirty years old with two college degrees, but she still found herself lapsing into fanciful thinking to get him back. She remembered once writing in her journal, "If there's a God as my mother believes, I'd like to strike a deal with Him: [I'll do] whatever it takes to go back in time and retrieve my son."

Simpson couldn't stand feeling so empty and sad. She wanted to hurry up and get pregnant again perhaps to replace the lost child, but also to undo her failure.

The grieving is of a different kind with adoption. Under this arrangement, your child is never entirely gone, although he or she is gone from your present life. There is enormous guilt: did I do the right thing? Will the child understand when he or she is a grown-up? Will the adoptive parents treat him or her well? There are feelings of longing (for what cannot be), regret (guilt), resignation ("There was nothing else I could do"), and relief ("Now I can get on with my life"). Of course, as mentioned earlier, guilt is usually mixed in with relief, as if you should not feel good about something so bad.

GIVING UP YOUR BABY FOR ADOPTION

Teenage fathers can feel any of the above feelings, too. In general, there is a three-month lag with men in the recognition of a pregnancy. Men often do not conceptualize the pregnancy (although they rationally accept it) until it is a visible thing, usually in the second trimester. Most miscarriages take place in the first trimester, so the man may not have the awareness or bond that the woman has.

There seems to be an element of shock and disbelief, especially with teenagers. The surprise of becoming pregnant in the first place ("I didn't think it could happen to us") gives way to the shock of death in this day and age ("She did everything right; so how could something like this have happened?").

After her son's death, Simpson initially thought her husband hated her. She thought he blamed her for their son's death, that he probably couldn't stand being around her. She even had fantasies that he wanted to leave her until she gradually realized that it was she who was doing all the hating and blaming. All the horrible thoughts she attributed to him were really things she was feeling about herself. Once she accepted that, she could see through to her husband's grief and include him in her struggle to get beyond the loss.

In most cases, society is less responsive to men who have lost children, seeming to view the early loss as the woman's misfortune. And as mentioned, society sees it as almost no loss at all to an unwed teenager.

How do you prevent losses such as miscarriages and stillbirths? Well, unfortunately, you can't prevent all of them. Some pregnancies are meant to be lost because something is wrong with the developing fetus. Some things are simply unexplainable or beyond your control. Aside from that, what you can do to ensure a healthy pregnancy is to receive prompt prenatal care and avoid all substances dangerous to the fetus. How do you cope with a loss? For one thing, you must recognize and acknowledge your feelings, whatever they may be (which means feeling them, not simply naming the feelings; there's a difference). Let yourself feel whatever it is you're feeling, not what society tells you to feel, and not even necessarily what has been mentioned here. Sometimes it is useful to keep a journal of your feelings. Putting your feelings on paper has a purging effect.

The next step is to talk about it with a concerned adult or a peer. Sharing your feelings is a way of sorting them out, getting some perspective, and sharing the pain.

If your baby dies in the hospital, there are ways to lessen the trauma of your hospital stay. The nursing staff should already have separated you from the other new mothers so that you won't have to cope with the sights and sounds of motherhood. If they have not done so and it bothers you to be near the newborns, ask the staff to move you. You have that right. Seek out the nurses who may be hesitant to approach you about your loss. They are there to talk with you, not just monitor your blood pressure, and they are usually familiar with infant death.

Following her son's stillbirth, Simpson was in the hospital for an additional twenty-four hours. Fortunately, she had a private room in the gynecological wing (where everyone was having tubal ligations or hysterectomies), so she didn't have to deal with other new mothers cooing over infants. Everything went smoothly until she was leaving. Then the nurse escorting Simpson out caught an elevator that was already heading down. She rolled Simpson into that elevator before they noticed the other occupants: a nurse behind the wheelchair of a young mother and newborn. Simpson stared straight ahead at the control buttons and willed herself to keep breathing during the eight floors it took to get down. They exited together—that young woman with her daughter, and she with her son's stillbirth certificate. It was just one of those things.

Sometimes it is important to view and have a service for the dead child, if he or she was stillborn or died shortly after birth. Depending on how you feel, sometimes having the fetus of a miscarriage buried puts some closure on the event. In any case, a professional should discuss the options with you and support you but not take over for you if it can be avoided. You were capable of becoming pregnant and being a mother; you are capable of handling the death.

If you are choking on anger, and most people are at some point, the best thing to do is to mobilize all that emotion. Find an appropriate channel by doing the following:

1. Joining a peer support group to meet others facing what you've been through. (You can find these through your YWCA, school, or house of worship.)
2. Taking up a sport or hobby.
3. Setting some positive short-term goal and working toward it. Getting pregnant again is not one of them. It is better to mourn your loss and prepare for a healthy pregnancy later than to jump back into a pregnancy too soon.

You will feel sad. There's no way around that. Some experts say that grieving lasts six months. There is probably no specific time period because people's ability to handle tragedy differs greatly. But if you are still finding it impossible to get out of bed in the morning several months after the loss, or if you are abusing drugs or alcohol to dull the pain, you need professional help. If you are wondering, "Why bother going on with life at all?" you need professional help at once. Professionals are trained to help people deal with the painful stages of recovery, and they can help you—no matter what your ability to pay for the therapy. The next chapter describes some of the various kinds of counselors.

You can cope if you follow a few bits of advice. If you're sad, the worst thing you can do is bottle it up. Instead, talk to adults and peers. If you are seriously depressed or suicidal, call a counseling agency, the hospital, your guidance counselor, your minister, or all of the above. Don't be in a hurry to get pregnant again. You have plenty of time to conceive when circumstances are better and you are not trying to replace the lost child.

Last of all, no one can guarantee that the pain will go away, but you can live through it. Many people have.

CHAPTER 14

GETTING COUNSELING OR THERAPY

It is not unusual to be depressed after suffering a loss in pregnancy. Some women bounce back after grieving, but many others have trouble with the grieving process. They may show signs of clinical depression, sleep too much, obsess about the loss, cry throughout the day, and even feel suicidal.

Even girls who have successful labors and deliveries can feel overwhelmed by the responsibilities of motherhood or their changing hormone levels. They, too, may show signs of clinical depression. When anyone continues to suffer depressive symptoms for more than two weeks, professional help is needed.

Finding the right therapist can seem as confusing as the problems propelling you into counseling in the first place. Briefly, this chapter will examine how the five main types of therapists differ, how you can go about selecting one with whom you're comfortable, and what you can expect therapy to do for you.

A psychiatrist is not only a therapist but a medical doctor as well. That means only this person can prescribe medicine for you if your problem requires the use of medication. A licensed psychiatrist has completed medical school and has earned a state medical license (usually requiring passage of an examination and a year of internship). Many psychiatrists have completed three additional years of residency in psychiatry, for a total of four years of graduate work after medical school.

Now what does that mean to you? Well, if you require medical attention for the treatment of severe depression, for example, you might be referred to a psychiatrist. It is costly—it can be $100 or more an hour. Reputable psychiatrists, however, are affiliated with counseling agencies as well as having private practice, so you can often see them at reduced fees. However, you do not need a psychiatrist simply because you believe that a specialist is the cream of the crop of the medical profession. Many other professionals are equally qualified to help you, and if they judge that you need the expertise of a psychiatrist, they can work in conjunction with one in your treatment.

A psychologist is also a doctor but cannot prescribe medicine. Usually, a psychologist has either a Ph.D. (doctorate in psychology) or an Ed.D. (doctorate in education and counseling) and has had four to five years of college at the graduate level. To be licensed, he or she must have had an additional two years of supervised counseling experience. Like psychiatrists, he or she can belong to organizations that monitor his or her behavior. Those organizations are to your benefit, of course. A psychologist can administer tests to assess a person's strengths and weaknesses and has the knowledge to interpret and use the results. Naturally, a psychologist is expensive unless seen at a clinic, which can reduce the fees based on your ability to pay, but this in no way means that the quality of care will be compromised.

Social workers are often thought of as people who dole out welfare checks and then follow up to make sure you spend the money wisely. Well, there are other kinds of social workers who are trained as counselors. As a matter of fact, social workers are now the primary providers of mental health treatment. They do more counseling than psychologists or psychiatrists. To be licensed, a social worker must have a master's in social work (MSW) and have completed two years of postgraduate study and two years of supervised practice. Some social workers hold a doctorate, too. In most states, they must pass a written exam. Social workers, like their colleagues in psychiatry and psychology, can be seen in private practice or in clinics for reduced fees. Their individual differences reflect more their specialization in practice than their inherent ability.

A fourth group of professionals have backgrounds in the counseling field but not specifically in social work or clinical psychology. If these people take the required counseling courses, pass a national licensing exam, and receive two years of supervision counseling others, they receive licensure as a licensed professional counselor, or LPC. Their roles are similar to those of clinical social workers. Some also have experience in administering and interpreting psychological tests.

In addition, there are psychiatric nurses, often called clinical nurse specialists. They have a degree in nursing (preferably a BS), plus a master's in psychiatric and mental health nursing or in counseling. They must pass a state licensing examination to practice as a professional registered nurse, and after two years of postgraduate experience, they may take the exam for certification as a clinical specialist. You can find clinical nurse specialists in a clinic setting or working in private practice with a doctor. Their fees vary.

That is a quick rundown on the people who are qualified to help you by virtue of their mental health training. Of course, there are also religious leaders trained in counseling and substance abuse counselors who may not have postgraduate training. There are also people who call themselves counselors, though they have no visible evidence of having earned the title. Some of these people may indeed be helpful, but you have little recourse if they prove disreputable.

Being depressed or distraught, you're probably not in a position to comparison shop for a therapist. Your best course is to find a comprehensive mental health clinic (one that offers a variety of services) and ask for an appointment.

The first thing to consider (if you're relying on your insurance, or your parents' insurance, to pay for treatment) is whether it is part of your HMO (health maintenance organization) or covered by your insurance carrier.

Sometimes you have little choice when it comes to what agency you see (or what group of counselors), but you should have some say about whom you can see within the group to which you are assigned.

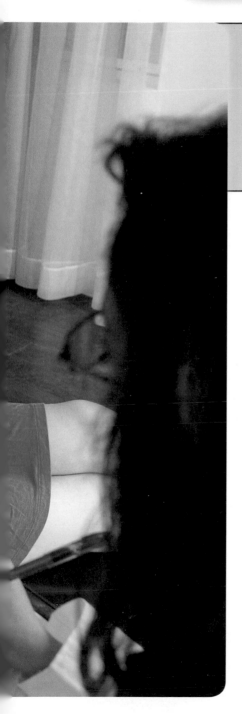

When choosing a therapist, make sure that the professional is licensed and that you feel comfortable talking to him or her. Therapy is difficult work, but in the end you will be able to move forward with your life and learn the skills for working on your depression.

Often the intake worker (the first person you speak with at length) is not the one who will continue to handle your case. You can always request someone else if you wish. Most important, you will want to know that the people you see are licensed, not only for your own peace of mind but also because insurance companies will not, as a rule, reimburse you for services of unlicensed counselors.

Second, you need to consider the cost, particularly if you do not have insurance. The kind of therapist you see is not as important as whether you are comfortable with the person (which does not mean you have to like the person all the time).

Simpson spent several months struggling over divorce issues with her first therapist. She hated going to therapy and always felt great relief when the weekly session was over. She thought up ingenious ways to miss appointments. Finally, it dawned on her that she could not relate to this woman and she might do better with someone else. All they seemed to do was fight over Simpson's desire to be in therapy, and her reasons for seeking therapy in the first place had taken a backseat.

You might also consider how available the person can be. If you find yourself seeing someone who is in town only once every two weeks, you'll be doing a lot of work on your own.

You do not need to like your therapist. The important thing is that you listen and he or she listens—that you respect each other.

Working through painful issues is difficult. In other words, you're not supposed to come away feeling as if everything has been resolved in one session. Often it takes months or more of steady workdays of feeling that you've made a step forward, followed by days when you've fallen two steps back. It evens out in the end if you don't give up too quickly. Simpson's experience has been that young people (or anyone, for that matter) give up when the sessions become painful. Then they are left with despair, and nothing further is resolved. Therapy is hard work.

Realize that not all therapists get along equally with everyone. Your best friend may recommend a woman she thinks is the kindest person in the world. But you may see that therapist as a badgering, mean-spirited old woman. No matter. Talk to the badgering, mean-spirited old woman and tell her you think you two have a problem. Then you both can work out whether you need someone else as a therapist or you're just using personalities as a way of getting around treatment.

Simpson once had a client who told her at the end of their hour that she was the best therapist she'd ever had, that Simpson had helped her so much that she would be eternally grateful. While Simpson was patting herself on the back, her next client marched in for her appointment. She informed Simpson that if Simpson didn't get her act together and soon, she would have to quit seeing her. Simpson's ego came crashing back to earth.

What can you expect therapy to do for you? First of all, you may initially feel relieved that you've found someone with whom to work on your depression. But therapy is a complicated process whereby you usually get better only by first getting worse. That sounds contradictory, but it really isn't. Sifting through the bad things in your life, you are likely to become more depressed until (with the therapist's help) you find your way out of the mess. Even a well-credentialed therapist is no guarantee that you will get better. A psychologist once told Simpson that if you sat a client in a therapist's office and the two of them simply read the phone book together, chances are the client would improve. That's because people often feel better when they have someone with whom to share problems. Nonetheless, you should come to feel you have greater control over your emotions and life. If that is not happening, reexamine what propelled you into counseling in the first place. Sometimes it's hard to realize that you *are* better.

Certain things are unethical in treatment. A reputable therapist will never initiate or accept sexual advances. If your therapist cannot maintain this boundary with you, get out of treatment and report it. Sex between client and therapist is not meant to happen. Why? Because in the long run it will only hurt you, confuse you, and make you dependent on the therapist in an unhealthy way. The reputable therapist knows this fact. That does not mean you won't be sexually attracted to your therapist; that may very well happen. It simply means that he or she is bound by ethics not to act on sexual feelings.

Last of all, realize that it is not a measure of your character if you need to see someone to help you through a crisis. Sometimes it requires more strength to seek help than it does to bury the problem.

There are plenty of people out there who can help you. It's mostly a matter of finding someone you are comfortable with, someone who is reputable and ethical and willing to listen.

And like everyone, some have better days than others.

Simpson can't remember exactly how old she was when she first realized that she was no longer the center of attention in her family. The limelight left her gradually, and after a while, she could get nowhere just by flashing her dimples. Simpson thinks she stopped being "cute" around the time her younger brother made his entrance into the world. After Mark was born, she was supposed to be satisfied with being the big sister. She never got much out of being older except more responsibility— and she certainly got away with less. To this day, Simpson remembers when that same baby brother ran out the front door, down the walk, and right into the street. Who got punished for leading her parents on a merry chase down the center of the highway? She did, of course, because she was the one who had not spotted Mark climbing over the barricade by the front door. Mark was still the center of attention, and she got sent to bed early!

Age and size can have their disadvantages.

It may be hard to believe, but motherhood involves growing up and losing the limelight. Many pregnant teenagers also lose their chance to create a better life for themselves. Perhaps having struggled in a household where parents or stepparents brought them up, some teenagers may have hoped they could make a more stable

Although this teen mom has made the care of her child a priority, she is completing her high school requirements so that she can receive a diploma. She understands that she now must be responsible for a life besides her own.

life for themselves. But instead of using their education or a job as the means to propel themselves beyond the home, they chose boyfriends and motherhood.

Given that teenage motherhood is so difficult, girls more often than not lose their chance to improve their circumstances. In no time, they have a baby to care for and a husband. If there is no husband, they are either more entrenched in their family or they turn to welfare, which at best is only a meager way of living. Motherhood, under these circumstances, brings additional hardship and lost opportunities.

Motherhood also means a loss of control over certain parts of your life. First, during the pregnancy you feel that your

body is no longer your own and your emotions are out of control. Your body does its own thing during labor. After delivery, everything you do is second in line to this baby. Being responsible for a child who is totally dependent on you can make your life feel out of control.

One of the most startling discoveries you make is that now you are responsible for another human being. Whereas you may have been the center of attention during the pregnancy, now the baby takes center stage. It's worse than simply growing up because not only are you out of the limelight, but you also have become one of those often misunderstood creatures—a mother. Remember what you thought of your own?

Simpson said she can't remember just when it dawned on her that her innocent little baby would one day consider her as old and outdated as her own parents appeared to her. Somehow, after pregnancy, she had become one of "them." She had to be serious and responsible. She had to worry about paying the bills on time or just paying them period. She had to make a will and name a guardian for her child. She had to prepare three meals each day, even when she didn't feel like eating anything more than a salad. After all, she was a mother now, and this baby was depending on her to behave like one.

Like any major life event, motherhood brings trade-offs. There are good things, like the joy of raising another human being and the opportunity to give and receive love. But there are losses, too, and if you fail to recognize them, you risk building up years of anger and resentment.

A young mother and her son play on the floor at home. Although there are big adjustments that must be made in a teen mother's life, raising another human being and being able to love him or her and receive love back are exhilarating.

These losses are hard to see—the loss of your own childhood, independence and sense of control over your life, freedom, and sometimes choices.

The most profound joy—that of loving another human being—is also the most frightening. The day Simpson's infant daughter was hospitalized for a severe case of jaundice, Simpson felt her insides plunge to her feet. She thought she would die if something happened to her. Suddenly, she had a picture of her own parents waving good-bye to her as she left home for the first time so many years earlier.

"How did they ever let me go?" Simpson wondered, when she was having this much trouble just handing her baby over to the nurse. The burden of caring so much for another human being crashed onto her shoulders.

You, as teenagers, are just past being children yourselves. How much more have you given up by cutting your own childhood short to become parents?

To recognize what you have lost means knowing what you have gained. In the end, hopefully, you'll be able to say it was a fair trade-off.

The best way to avoid getting pregnant is to practice sexual abstinence, which means to refrain from having sex. However, if you do plan to have sex, you should always use contraception, also known as birth control. It not only prevents pregnancy, but some birth control methods can also protect you from sexually transmitted diseases (STDs).

It is a myth that you cannot conceive again after delivery until you have had a period. It is equally untrue that you cannot get pregnant while you are nursing. Haven't you noticed in school that some of the kids in the same family are only a year apart in age? How do you think that happened?

If you are unconcerned about getting pregnant again because you think a family member will raise another baby, you have already demonstrated that you are too immature to be engaging in sex in the first place. The mature person, whether a teenager or a woman in her thirties, knows that sex implies responsibility—knowing how to protect herself not only from unplanned pregnancies but from STDs as well.

If you went to a family planning clinic during your previous pregnancy, you were probably given contraceptive information. If you are not involved with a clinic, you should talk with your doctor about the various methods of birth control.

BIRTH CONTROL PILLS

To obtain birth control pills, you need a doctor's prescription. You need to visit a doctor to have a physical exam to determine that you have no physical problems that would make taking the pill dangerous for you. Some birth control pills contain estrogen and progestin, two hormones, and these pills are called combination pills. Other pills are progestin-only pills. The majority of women take combination pills. The pills' hormones keep a woman's ovaries from releasing eggs (ovulation).

Although the pill is convenient to use (you take one pill each day of the month, excluding the week you are menstruating) and does not interfere with the sexual experience, it does have certain drawbacks.

Pros and Cons

Some of the advantages and disadvantages of taking birth control pills include the following:

The side effects can include nausea, vomiting, and weight gain. Depending on one's medical history, not everyone can take the pill safely.

The pill will not protect you against STDs or HIV/AIDS. You must be 100 percent sure of your partner's sexual history before relying solely on the pill. The only antibiotic known to interfere with the pill is rifampin, used to treat tuberculosis. All other medications have been proven not to interfere with the pill. Always tell your doctor what other medications you are taking, though.

You must be familiar with the instructions for taking the pill, and you must take the pill consistently. If you experience sickness, and especially if you're vomiting, be sure to use a backup method of birth control because you are probably not keeping down the amount of hormone needed to prevent pregnancy. If your body cannot handle the pill after a trial period, ask your doctor for either a change in the dosage or another method of birth control. Remember, the pill is almost 100 percent effective only when taken consistently. If you cannot remember to take the pill every day, this method isn't right for you.

ANOTHER CONTRACEPTIVE: THE DIAPHRAGM

The diaphragm is relatively easy to use: you insert the shallow, latex cup-shaped diaphragm with a flexible rim into the vagina to cover the cervix and surrounding area. You need to have a health care professional prescribe and properly fit you for the diaphragm and show you how to insert and position it correctly. When combined with spermicidal cream or jelly (usually containing nonoxynol-9), a diaphragm has a failure rate of about fifteen pregnancies per one hundred women, according to the Office of Women's Health, in the Food and Drug Administration. The tricky part about the diaphragm is inserting it so that it covers the cervix properly.

ASK DR. JAN, PSYCHOLOGIST

First name: MB

Question:
I'd like to have sex with my boyfriend, but I don't know what kind of birth control to use. Do I have to get my parents' OK to go on birth control? And will others think I'm easy if I'm on birth control?

Answer:
You are smart to be thinking about birth control BEFORE having sex with your boyfriend, as one-third of all girls in the United States will get pregnant in their teen years. Whether or not you have access to birth control depends on the state in which you live. Twenty-one states (and Washington, D.C.) allow all minors access to contraceptive services, twenty-five states give minors access under specific conditions, and four states have no policy. To learn about the laws in your state, see: http://www.guttmacher.org/state center/spibs/spib_MACS.pdf.

In some states, there are also women's health clinics and/or teen health clinics that can provide health information to help you make informed decisions about using birth control and protecting yourself against sexually transmitted diseases. You can check with your local health department for more information.

Another option is to speak to your medical doctor. In some states, however, your doctor may, but is not required to, inform your parents.

It is always a good idea to speak to a trusted adult and seek his or her support in making these important decisions. It would be great if that person is a parent. If that's not possible, consider another adult in your home, school, or community.

Finally, it is tough to predict what others will think. What's more important is what you think. Make sure that you feel good about your behavior and are comfortable with the decisions you make.

Ask a Question

Do you have a question that you would like answered? E-mail your question to Dr. Jan at drjan@rosenpub.com. If your question is selected, it will appear on the Teen Health & Wellness Web site in "Dr. Jan's Corner."

If you have an urgent question on a health or wellness issue, we strongly encourage you to call a hotline to speak to a qualified professional or speak to a trusted adult, such as a parent, teacher, or guidance counselor. You can find hotlines listed in the For More Information section of this book, or at www. teenhealthandwellness.com/static/hotlines.

It is not meant to fit snugly over the cervix like the cervical cap, but if it is inserted haphazardly, it can serve as a gate, ushering the sperm right into the uterus. Make sure that a nurse has checked to see that you can insert the diaphragm properly before you leave the doctor's office.

It is also important to use a spermicidal jelly or cream with the diaphragm to increase its effectiveness. If sperm do get past the barrier of the diaphragm, the spermicide will kill them. Do not use petroleum jelly as a lubricant when using a diaphragm; an oil-based agent (such as

Vaseline or baby oil) will damage the diaphragm. It will eventually leak, and you know what that means. Use a water-based lubricant like K-Y jelly instead.

Pros and Cons

It should go without saying that the diaphragm is only as good as the person who uses it. Inserting a diaphragm after a few seconds of intercourse is a few seconds too late. Using it only at those times of the month you believe to be unsafe is irresponsible. No time is safe. It needs to be inserted up to six hours before having sex. Advantages include that it is reusable, relatively inexpensive, and easy to carry. Disadvantages include that you must use it every time you have sex, spermicidal agents can be messy, and sometimes urinary tract infections have occurred. You must leave the diaphragm in at least six hours after sex but no longer than twenty-four hours. Every time you remove the diaphragm, you must wash it and store it properly. If you have been pregnant or had weight loss or gain, you may need to be refitted for a new diaphragm. The diaphragm should be examined routinely for weakness or holes and replaced if damaged. Nevertheless, you should be fitted for a new diaphragm at least every two years.

There are a variety of contraceptives on the market today, including birth control pills, diaphragms, female and male condoms, birth control implants and shots, cervical caps, patches, IUDs, and rings, among others. Make certain that you discuss with your doctor the options that are best for you.

BIRTH CONTROL IMPLANT

An implantable rod, matchstick-sized, called Implanon, is inserted in a woman's upper arm to prevent pregnancy. It has to be implanted by a health care professional. Costing about $400 to $800, Implanon lasts around three years. It releases the hormone progestin, which keeps the ovaries from releasing eggs.

Pros and Cons

Some of the advantages of the implant include these: you don't have to worry about doing something every day, like taking a pill. The side effects are reportedly less severe than what you experience on the pill. If the implant is properly installed (and by the way, it doesn't hurt to have the implant), you will hardly notice that it's there. And, of course, the greatest advantage is its effectiveness—one out of one hundred women become pregnant each year while using Implanon.

Some of the disadvantages are: it is an expensive system. Certain medicines and supplements can make the implant less effective. The most common side effect is that it can cause irregular bleeding, particularly in the first six to twelve months of use. You may also not be a candidate for the implant—like all medications, there are some risks involved, so you should check with your health care professional to make sure Implanon is safe for you. Of course, it does nothing to prevent the transmission of sexually transmitted diseases, including HIV/AIDS. Finally, removal of the rod must be done by a health care provider.

THE INJECTION OR SHOT

The birth control shot, also called by the brand name Depo-Provera, is a shot given by a health care provider intramuscularly in your buttocks or upper arm every three months to prevent pregnancy. It is given during the first five days of your menstrual period. The shot contains medroxyprogesterone acetate, which is a derivative of the hormone progesterone. According to the FDA's Office of Women's Health, the shot is very effective— about one out of one hundred women will get pregnant each year if they always use the injection as directed.

Pros and Cons

Clearly, the greatest advantage of the Depo-Provera injection is that you do not need to worry about birth control all the time. There is no interruption to lovemaking, and there is no pill to remember to take.

The drawbacks include side effects (heavier-than-usual or missed menstrual periods; a lengthy time before regaining fertility) and contraindications (women who have had breast cancer, unexplained vaginal bleeding, or liver disease cannot use this method). Women may also lose bone mineral density, and the longer you use the shot, the greater the bone loss. It is also not known how the bone loss will affect adolescents later in life, if the injection is used in early adulthood. It is also recommended that the shot only be used as a long-term contraceptive (longer than two years) if other birth control options are not adequate. Another important consideration is that the shot does not protect you against STDs or HIV/AIDS.

THE FEMALE CONDOM

The plastic pouch that is used by women during sex is called the female condom, and it has flexible rings at each end. The female condom is inserted into the vagina right before sex. The ring at the closed end keeps the pouch in the vagina; the ring at the open end remains outside the vaginal opening during sex. The condom blocks sperm from entering the vagina.

Pros and Cons

Female condoms are fairly easy to obtain, and they help prevent infections. They can be used by people who are allergic to latex, and they can be used with oil-based and water-based lubricants. They have no effect on your natural hormones, and they do not require a prescription. Some people do not like the female condom because it can cause irritation to the vagina and penis.

THE MALE CONDOM

Another method—the male condom—is not only a good contraceptive but also the best means for some protection against some STDs and HIV/AIDS. It is important to buy condoms (also called rubbers or jimmies) made of latex because they prevent the spread of HIV/AIDS better than condoms made of animal skin. It is also important to use them before any sexual contact with your partner. It's equally important to withdraw after ejaculation and not let the condom slip off the penis. Any contact of bodily fluids can spread the HIV/AIDS virus if it is present. And, of course, sperm can swim into the vagina and through the fallopian tubes, even if they were deposited in a few drops at the entrance to the vagina. All it takes is one sperm and one egg to make a baby.

Spermicide should also be used with condoms—but not in the condom itself, which can cause it to slip off. Follow the package instructions.

Pros and Cons

A word about nonoxynol-9: It is the most effective ingredient in killing sperm, but it can be abrasive, and many people are allergic to it. If you are one of the people who are allergic to this ingredient, talk to your doctor about substitutes.

Another thing—if you are turned off by all the fuss about inserting spermicides and wearing condoms, this is not the method for you. If people are uncomfortable with a procedure, they should not follow it. Birth control cannot be a halfhearted proposition. You either do it right or it won't work. It is unarguably messy to use spermicide and condoms, and it requires forethought to insert your diaphragm and remember the condom. (By the way, do not carry condoms in your wallet. The heat from your body will destroy them.)

THE CERVICAL CAP

Also called the FemCap, the cervical cap is a silicone cup that is inserted into the vagina, over the cervix. Used with a spermicide cream or jelly, the cap keeps sperm from joining with an egg by blocking the opening to the uterus. According to the FDA Office of Women's Health, between seventeen to twenty-three women will become pregnant out of one hundred who use this method of birth control.

Pros and Cons

The cervical cap is convenient to use, and it's easy to carry. It also has no effect on a woman's natural hormones, and it can be used if you are nursing a child. Disadvantages include: You can't use it during your period, it can be difficult to insert, it must be used every time you have sex, and you may need to be refitted after you've been pregnant.

THE PATCH

The birth control patch, also called Ortho Evra after its brand name, is a thin plastic patch, beige in color, that sticks to the skin. A new patch is placed on the skin once each week, for three weeks in a row. The next week is without a patch. The patch works by releasing hormones into the body. Just like the pill, the patch releases estrogen and progestin, which keep you from ovulating.

Pros and Cons

The patch is easy to use. According to Planned Parenthood, "Many women who use the patch have more regular, lighter, and shorter periods." Because it works similarly to the pill, the patch has some of the same benefits. And, likewise, it probably has similar disadvantages, including such side effects as bleeding between periods and nausea and vomiting. It is important to note that the patch is a very controversial option, especially for young women, because of the risk of stroke or blood clots. There have been numerous lawsuits against a manufacturer of the patch, and many doctors have stopped prescribing the patch to their patients. It's essential that you discuss with your doctor whether he or she thinks the patch is a good option for you. The patch does not protect a woman from STDs or HIV/AIDS.

THE RING

The vaginal ring (also called NuvaRing) is a small, flexible ring that you insert into your vagina once each month to prevent pregnancy. It's left in place for three weeks and then removed for the remaining week each month. The ring releases hormones, which prevent ovulation. You need to get a prescription from a health care provider and discuss whether this is a likely option of birth control for you. Usually, you start using the ring within the first five days after the onset of your period. If you insert it later than that, protection begins after seven days, so you had better use another method of birth control if you have sex during the first week of your use of the ring.

Pros and Cons

The ring is simple to use. The ring has benefits and disadvantages that are similar to that of the pill. If you are breast-feeding, you should wait until after nursing to use the ring because it could affect the quality of mother's milk. (In addition, breast milk will contain traces of the ring's hormones, although there may not be any effect of the hormones on your baby.)

IUD

The intrauterine device, or IUD, is a small, T-shaped device made of plastic. This birth control method is generally not recommended for use by teens. One brand contains copper and is effective in preventing pregnancy for about twelve years. Another brand releases progestin and is effective for about five years. The IUD prevents sperm from joining the egg, and it is one of the most effective methods of birth control—one woman will become pregnant out of one hundred women using the device. You need to visit a health care professional to obtain an IUD and have it inserted.

Pros and Cons

The IUD is a long-lasting form of contraceptive, considering some of the other options. It is relatively stress-free and often reduces menstrual flow. On the downside, the IUD can cause moderate pain when it is first inserted. Some women have cramps and backaches for a while afterward. Sometimes an IUD can slip out of the uterus, and pregnancy can happen if it's not in properly. In rare cases, a woman can get an infection when using an IUD. Other complications can occur if the IUD pushes through the wall of the uterus. So make sure you pay attention to any symptoms you might have once you have gotten an IUD.

EMERGENCY CONTRACEPTION

Also called the morning-after pill, emergency contraception can be used to prevent pregnancy up to five days after having unprotected sex. This emergency birth control is used when your other form of birth control failed (condom broke, or you forgot to take the pill, insert your ring, or apply the patch), or if you were forced to have unprotected sex (rape). This pill releases hormones that stop ovulation. The Plan B One-Step and Next Choice brands of the pill are available at pharmacies and health centers without a prescription for women ages seventeen and older. If you are younger than seventeen, you'll need to go to a health care provider to obtain a prescription.

Pros and Cons

Emergency contraception is safe and does not have the same risks as taking the birth control pill. That's mainly because you won't be taking it long term. There are

Whatever method of birth control you and your partner choose, make sure you know how to use it properly and it protects you from STDs, such as AIDS.

some negative side effects, such as nausea and vomiting, dizziness, headaches, and irregular bleeding.

There are other methods of birth control, such as natural birth control. This involves temperature taking and mucus reading. This method is not discussed here because a teenager's menstrual cycle is not regular enough for it to be reliable. Whatever method you choose, you need to consider many circumstances before making a decision. According to the Mayo Clinic, these factors include "your age, health, emotional maturity, marital status, and religious convictions." You and your partner should consider the choices that work best for both of you.

THE RISKS OF STDS AND HIV/AIDS

If you are convinced that you will remember to use the pill, you must be doubly sure of your partner's health. HIV/AIDS is not something that happens only to adults, gay men, and drug users. Teenagers constitute the fastest-growing segment of the population with HIV infection because they are the people who least anticipate it and thus fail to take precautions against it. You are always susceptible when you don't know whether your partner uses drugs or needles or has engaged in past sexual behavior, and especially if you have multiple partners yourself. AIDS can kill you. There is no cure for it. There is no such thing as safe sex. Abstinence is the only sure-fire method. AIDS kills indiscriminately. An unplanned pregnancy may change your life, but it won't take it. AIDS will.

Sexually transmitted diseases (STDs) can also make you ill. Male and female condoms can offer some reliable protection from STDs. When left untreated, some STDs can lead to sterility. It is hard for teenagers to consider the consequences of their behavior when the results might not show up for several years. But this is another time when you have to use common sense. STDs do not go away by themselves; they must be medically treated, and you must inform any partners so that they can also be treated. In the long run, it is better to prevent the diseases than try to minimize the damage after it has been done. (If you wind up pregnant on top of contracting an STD, the disease seriously complicates your delivering a healthy baby.)

Before you have a second child, place yourself in the best circumstances possible: have a stable home life; a secure, well-paying job; and time and energy enough to devote to another baby. Remember, you would not be trading this first child in for the baby. You would have two babies at home, with twice the demands for your attention. And your first child may resent your paying attention to the second child.

An unexpected pregnancy will not happen the second time if you take responsibility for preventing it. That means that you, the woman, need either to invest in the long-term birth control options (the injection, the implant, the pill, the IUD) or plan to use birth control devices each and every time you engage in sex. Because you're the one who will go through the pregnancy, labor, and delivery, you need to be certain that it will not happen again before you are ready. If your partner relies on condoms but does not always supply them, you need to buy some and keep them on hand.

THE GUY'S VIEWPOINT

If you, the guy, do not want the financial responsibility of another child, you need to be certain your partner is using birth control. If you're not sure she is taking the

MYTHS AND FACTS

MYTH

I can't get pregnant the first time I have sex.

FACT

Yes, you can. The female body is at its most fertile during the teens and early twenties, so there's no guarantee that the first sexual contact will be safe. Proper birth control should be used from the very beginning of sexual activity.

MYTH

I can't get pregnant if I have my period.

FACT

Yes, you can get pregnant if you have vaginal sex during your period. Considering that sperm can survive inside of you anywhere from a day to almost a week, you should be using some method of birth control even during this time. STDs can be transmitted during this time, too, so a condom is always the safest method and should always be used if you're sleeping with someone who you are not absolutely positive does not have an STD.

MYTH

Forgetting to take my pill for one day will increase my risk of pregnancy.

FACT

Not necessarily. Follow the directions from your prescription. In most cases, you will be instructed to take two pills the following day.

1. Do I need to use a backup method in addition to my hormonal contraceptive?

2. Why have my periods stopped? Should I take a pregnancy test?

3. I took the pill before I knew I was pregnant. Can the hormones hurt my baby?

4. Can I take the pill safely with my other medicines?

5. Which birth control method do you recommend?

6. If the condom is recommended, which is more effective—the male or female condom?

7. What should be done if the condom breaks during intercourse without our knowledge?

8. Can I have a prescription for emergency contraception, just in case I need it?

9. Do all contraceptives have side effects?

10. Do novelty condoms (i.e. colored, glow in the dark, ribbed ticklers) provide the same protection against sexually transmitted diseases and pregnancy that regular condoms do?

10 GREAT QUESTIONS TO ASK YOUR DOCTOR

pill or is up to date on her shots, plan to use condoms each time you engage in sex. Remember, there really is no safe time.

Both of you have a responsibility to prevent another pregnancy until you are in a position to provide for another child. But more than that, both of you have an obligation to each other to protect yourselves from STDs, including HIV/AIDS. By waiting to have another baby, you are making the right choice for yourself, your partner, and your child.

ABOUT DR. JAN

Dr. Jan Hittelman is a licensed psychologist with over twenty years of experience working with teens, children, adults, and families in a variety of settings.

In addition to clinical practices in California, Colorado, and New York, he has specialized in program development in partnership with school systems, psychiatric hospitals, correctional facilities and the courts, outpatient settings, residential treatment facilities, and private nonprofit organizations.

He founded Compass House, a nonprofit counseling collaborative for teens and their families. He launched Boulder Psychological Services in 2007.

Dr. Hittelman also authors a monthly newspaper column entitled "Surviving the Teenage Years" in the *Boulder Daily Camera*, writes monthly columns for the Boulder Valley School District under the sponsorship of the Parent Engagement Network, and publishes an online question-and-answer column for teens in the Rosen Publishing Group's online resource Teen Health & Wellness.

Teen Health & Wellness: Real Life, Real Answers (*http://www.teenhealthandwellness.com*) is a database designed for teens on issues relating to health, fitness, alcohol, drugs, mental health, family life, and much more. Check your school or local library for access.

GLOSSARY

abstinence The practice of restraining oneself from having sex.

anemic Suffering from anemia, a deficiency of red blood cells, which makes a person weak, listless, and tired.

colostrum Milk secreted during pregnancy and for a few days after childbirth that is high in protein and antibodies.

contraindication A condition that makes a particular treatment or procedure inadvisable.

epidural block Also called an epidural, an injection of pain medication that is often given in the lower back of a woman during labor or right before a Cesarean section for pain relief.

fetal alcohol effect (FAE) A syndrome characterized by numerous developmental and behavioral problems in infants whose mothers drank moderate amounts of alcohol during pregnancy.

fetal alcohol syndrome (FAS) A highly variable group of birth defects including mental retardation, deficient growth, and malformations of the skull and face that tend to occur in the infants of women who consumed large amounts of alcohol during pregnancy.

foster care A formal system by which a child is cared for by people other than his or her own parents, but without having been adopted.

hormone A chemical that is produced in an organism and is transported in tissue fluids such as blood to stimulate specific cells to begin or stop a function.

human chorionic gonadotropin Abbreviated as HCG, a hormone that is produced early in pregnancy by the placenta. The detection of HCG in urine and serum is the basis for one type of pregnancy test.

irrevocable Not able to be changed or reversed; final.

Lamaze Relating to a method of childbirth that involves exercises and breath control to give pain relief without medications.

miscarriage The expulsion of a fetus from the womb before it is able to survive independently.

MMR vaccine A three-in-one vaccine that protects against measles, mumps, and rubella, which can be serious diseases during childhood.

neonatal Of or relating to newborn children.

ovulation The discharge of a mature ovum (egg) from the ovary.

postpartum After childbirth.

prenatal Before birth; during or relating to pregnancy.

rubella Also called German measles, a contagious viral disease with symptoms similar to mild measles. It can cause malformation of a fetus if contracted in early pregnancy.

stillbirth The birth of a baby that has died in the womb.

sudden infant death syndrome (SIDS) The death of a seemingly healthy baby in its sleep, due to a cessation of breathing.

FOR MORE INFORMATION

Adoption Council of Canada (ACC)
211 Bronson Avenue
Ottawa, ON K1R 6H5
Canada
(613) 235-0344
Web site: http://www.adoption.ca

The ACC is the umbrella organization for adoption in Canada. It raises public awareness of adoption, promotes placement of waiting children, and stresses the importance of post-adoption services.

American Pregnancy Association
1431 Greenway Drive, Suite 800
Irving, TX 75038
(972) 550-0140
Web site: http://www.american pregnancy.org

This national health organization promotes reproductive and pregnancy wellness through its education, research, and community awareness programs.

America's Pregnancy Helpline
(888) 672-2296
Web site: http://www.thehelpline.org

America's Pregnancy Helpline is a national health organization committed to ongoing reproductive research and education, promoting community awareness, and providing fact-based information for women and families with pregnancy-related needs.

Birthright Hotline
(800) 550-4900
Web site: http://www.birthright.org

Birthright International is the world's first international crisis pregnancy service. It operates a twenty-four-hour North American hotline. Birthright takes a "non-moralistic, non-judgmental" approach toward helping women through their pregnancy challenges.

Campaign for Our Children (CFOC)
One North Charles Street, Suite 1100
Baltimore, MD 21201
(410) 576-9015
Web site: http://www.cfoc.org

The Campaign for Our Children addresses high teen birth rates through a comprehensive, hands-on program to educate children, parents, and the general public. The CFOC's materials have been incorporated into adolescent prevention programs, schools, and community organizations in all fifty states.

Canadian Paediatric Society
2305 Saint Laurent Boulevard
Ottawa, ON K1G 4J8
Canada
(613) 526-9397
Web site: http://www.cps.ca

This society is the Canadian association of pediatricians, committed to working together and with others to advance the health of children and youth by promoting excellence in health care, advocacy, education, research, and support of its membership.

Centers for Disease Control and Prevention (CDC)

1600 Clifton Road
Atlanta, GA 30333
(800) 232-4636
Web site: http://www.cdc.gov

This federal agency is the primary division for obtaining information on health and safety issues for the general public. Its Web site contains educational information about reproductive health and children's issues.

ETR's Resource Center for Adolescent Pregnancy Prevention (ReCAPP)

Web site: http://www.etr.org/recapp

The ETR is a private, nonprofit health-education promotion organization based in Santa Cruz, California. It offers state-of-the-art programs, professional training, and research in the area of adolescent pregnancy prevention.

Guttmacher Institute

125 Maiden Lane, 7th Floor
New York, NY 10038
(800) 355-0244
Web site: http://www.guttmacher.org

This organization advances sexual and reproductive health globally by offering research, public education, and policy analysis programs.

Health Resources and Services Administration (HRSA)

U.S. Department of Health and Human Services
5600 Fishers Lane

Rockville, MD 20857
(888) 275-4772
Web site: http://www.hrsa.gov

The HRSA supports programs and offers grants to improve the health of needy people.

National Campaign to Prevent Teen Pregnancy

1776 Massachusetts Avenue NW, Suite 200
Washington, DC 20036
(202) 478-8500
Web site: http://www.teenpregnancy.org

The National Campaign to Prevent Teen Pregnancy is a nonprofit initiative whose mission is to improve the well-being of children, youth, and families by reducing teen pregnancy.

National Women's Health Network

514 Tenth Street NW, Suite 400
Washington, DC 20005
(202) 347-1140
Web site: http://www.nwhn.org

The National Women's Health Network is committed to improving the health of all women by developing and promoting a critical analysis of health issues to affect policy and support consumer decision making.

Office of Family Assistance

Administration for Children and Families
370 L'Enfant Promenade SW
Washington, DC 20447
(202) 401-9275
Web site: http://www.acf.hhs.gov

This federal office administers the Temporary Assistance for Needy Families (TANF) program.

Parenting Questions and Answers

Web site: http://www.parenting-qa.com

Parenting-qa.com provides a resource for parents to get help with many of the questions that will arise when raising children. The articles and answers to questions on this site are provided by parents from across the country.

Parents Anonymous, Inc.

675 West Foothill Boulevard, Suite 220

Claremont, CA 91711-3475

(909) 621-6184

Helpline: (800) 843-5437

The nation's oldest child abuse prevention organization, Parents Anonymous works to provide families with safe and nurturing homes for all children.

Planned Parenthood Federation of America

434 West 33rd Street

New York, NY 10001

(800) 230-7526

Web site: http://www.plannedparenthood.org

Planned Parenthood provides comprehensive reproductive and related health care services in settings that preserve and protect the privacy and rights of each individual.

Sexuality Information and Education Council of the United States (SIECUS)

130 West 42nd Street

New York, NY 10036
(212) 819-9770
Web site: http://www.siecus.org

SIECUS is a national voice for sexuality education, sexual health, and sexual rights. It advocates for the right of all people to accurate information, comprehensive education about sexuality, and sexual health services.

WEB SITES

Due to the changing nature of Internet links, Rosen Publishing has developed an online list of Web sites related to the subject of this book. This site is updated regularly. Please use this link to access this list:

http://www.rosenlinks.com/411/preg

FOR FURTHER READING

American Academy of Pediatrics. *Caring for Your Baby and Young Child: Birth to Age 5*. New York, NY: Random House Publishers, 2009.

Canfield, Jack, Mark Victor Hanson, Amy Newmark, and Madeline Clapps. *Chicken Soup for the Soul: Teens Talk High School: 101 Stories of Life, Love, and Learning for Older Teens*. Cos Cob, CT: Chicken Soup for the Soul, 2008.

Carlson-Berne, Emma. *Teen Pregnancy*. Farmington Hills, MI: Cengage Gale, 2006.

Davis, Deborah, ed. *You Look Too Young to Be a Mom*. New York, NY: Perigee Trade, 2004.

Ehrlich, J. Shoshanna. *Who Decides? The Abortion Rights of Teens* (Reproductive Rights and Policies). Santa Barbara, CA: Praeger, 2006.

Feinstein, Stephen. *Sexuality and Teens. What You Should Know About Sex, Abstinence, Birth Control, Pregnancy, and STDs*. Berkeley Heights, NJ: Enslow Publishers, 2009.

Frohnapfel-Krueger, Lisa. *Teen Pregnancy and Parenting* (Current Controversies). Farmington Hills, MI: Greenhaven Press, 2010.

Howard-Barr, Elissa, and Stacey M. Barrineau. *The Truth About Sexual Behavior and Unplanned Pregnancy*. New York, NY: Facts On File, 2009.

Hyde, Margaret O. *Safe Sex 101: An Overview for Teens* (Teen Overviews). Minneapolis, MN: Twenty-First Century Books, 2006.

Knowles, Jo. *Jumping Off Swings*. Somerville, MA: Candlewick Press, 2009.

Lindsay, Jeanne Warren. *Teen Dads: Rights, Responsibilities & Joys*. 3rd ed. Buena Park, CA: Morning Glory Press, 2008.

McDowell, Pamela. *Teen Pregnancy*. Vol. 6. New York, NY: Crabtree Publishing, 2010.

Roles, Patricia. *Facing Teenage Pregnancy: A Handbook for the Pregnant Teen*. 3rd ed. University Park, IL: Child Welfare League of America, 2006.

Williams, Heidi. *Teen Pregnancy* (Issues That Concern You). Farmington Hills, MI: Greenhaven Press, 2009.

Zonderman, Jon, and Laurel Shader. *Birth Control Pills* (Drugs: The Straight Facts). New York, NY: Chelsea House Publishers, 2006.

INDEX

A

B

C

D

ABOUT THE AUTHORS

Cleo Stanley is a writer who lives in Westchester County, New York.

Carolyn Simpson, a teacher, counselor, and writer, has worked in the mental health field since 1973. She received a bachelor's degree in sociology from Colby College, Waterville, Maine, and a master's degree in human relations from the University of Oklahoma, Norman, Oklahoma.

She worked as a clinical social worker for ten years, both in Maine and Oklahoma, and as a teacher and counselor in the Young Parent's Program serving pregnant teens in Bridgton, Maine. She has taught psychology at Tulsa Community College in Tulsa, Oklahoma, and has been an outpatient therapist at Parkside Behavioral Health Services in Tulsa.

PHOTO CREDITS

Cover, p. 1 Shutterstock.com; p. 4 Paul Costello/Stone/Getty Images; p. 10 © Mark Richards/PhotoEdit Inc.; pp. 13, 57, 71, 74 © AP Images; p. 22 © Bubbles Photolibrary/Alamy; p. 26 © www.istockphoto.com/sean boggs; p. 33 Michael Ferguson/ PHOTOlink.net/Newscom.com; p. 44 © Robin Laurance/Impact /HIP/The Image Works; pp. 46, 66, 84, 94, 206, 225 Courtesy of Jan S. Hittelman, Ph.D.; p. 59 Dick Schmidt/Sacramento Bee/ ZUMA Press; p. 78 © David Young-Wolff/PhotoEdit, Inc.; pp. 82, 150 MINDY SCHAUER/MCT/Newscom.com; pp. 88, 100, 160, 166–167, 192–193; p. 106 Thomas Barwick/Digital Vision/Getty Images; p. 116 Tina Stallard/Getty Images; pp. 124, 137, 146 Tina Stallard/Edit by Getty Images; p. 179 © www.istockphoto.com/ Elena Elisseeva; pp. 198–199 © Los Angeles Daily News/ZUMA Press; p. 201 © www.istockphoto.com/quavondo; p. 209 Charles Thatcher/Stone/Getty Images; pp. 218–219 William Wan/The Washington Post/Getty Images.

Photo Researcher: Amy Feinberg